Miraculous Saint of India

BHABA PAGLA

AF519485

NIRAMOY KHASNOBIS

BlueRose ONE.com
Stories Matter
NewDelhi • London

BLUEROSE PUBLISHERS
India | U.K.

BlueRose ONE.com
Stories Matter
NewDelhi • London

For permissions requests or inquiries regarding this publication,
please contact:

BLUEROSE PUBLISHERS
www.BlueRoseONE.com
info@bluerosepublishers.com
+91 8882 898 898
+4407342408967

ISBN: 978-93-5989-195-8

Cover design: Shivam
Typesetting: Namrata Saini

First Edition: February 2024

Message of Bhaba Pagla

01) HOW TO BE IMMORTAL? BY THINKING OF GOD AND HAVING FIRM BELIEF IN GOD.

02) WAITING GIVES A LOT OF THINGS, NEGLIGENCE LOSES ALL.

03) BOASTING OR PROUD IS NOT ORNAMENT, DECORATE THE BODY BY CHANTING "OHM". DISCUSSION OF SAINT AND GOOD WORDS ARE COMPANION OF YOURS

04) IF YOU ASK LIKE THAT YOU WILL NOT GET ANYTHING, INDULGE YOUR MIND INTO HIM TO WORSHIP HIM.

05) I LOVE PEOPLE, NO REQUIREMENT OF PILGRIMAGE; THE GAYA, GANGA, KASHI/ VARANASI.

06) I DON'T KNOW "THE KALI/TALI." DUTY IS MY GOD.

07) THE SOUL IS THE GREATEST SPIRITUAL MASTER. HOLD HIM FIRMLY, AND PERFORM YOUR DUTY BEFORE SITTING IN MEDITATION.

08) IF YOU WISH NOTHING IS DONE. IT REQUIRES THE WILL OF ICHYAMOYEE (GODDESS 'KALI")

09) MONEY IS REQUIRED IN THIS WORLD BUT SPIRITUAL OBJECT IS REQUIRED IN THAT WORLD.

10) DON'T FIGHT WITH ANYONE WHO IS ADVANCED A LITTLE BETTER.

11) YOU WILL NOT GET HIM BY THESE LESSONS, IT WILL BE OBTAINED BY HOLDING AND LAYING DOWN AT HIS FEET.

12) THE "KALI, KRISHNA, ALLAH, AND RASUL" ARE TIED IN THE SAME TUNE.

13) OH MAN, IF YOU WANT TO SEE GOD, SHUN YOUR NATURE OF VIOLENCE WHICH IS PRIME HINDRANCE.

14) KEEP YOUR MIND AT HIS FEET, YOU NEED NOT WORRY ABOUT THE WAYS.

15) IMITATION OF THOUGHT AND EMOTION ARE NOT PERMITTED, PRETENTION IS NOT WORSHIP.

16) BLACK BERRY PURIFIES BLOOD, THE NAME OF KALI (GODDESS) PURIFIES THE INNER SOUL.

17) I WILL FEAR HIM WHOM I GET NEAR ME BY MAKING HIM MY DEAR.

18) INVERT KALIMA" (GODDESS KALI), YOU WILL SEE THE CREATOR/MALIK OF THE WORLD.

19) LET PASSION, ANGER AND TEMPTATION ETC. ACCOMPANY YOU, LET IT BE REMAINED BUT NEVER FORGET THEIR TRICKS.

20) THE KRISHNA, KALI, SHIBARAM ARE NEVER DIFFERENT ALL TOGETHER, THE INSENSITIVE OF MIND; THOSE WHO DON'T UNDERSTAND ARE BLIND IN THEIR MIND. ~ SHRI SHRI TAKUR BHABAPAGLA.

21) DUTY IS MY GREAT RELIGION, ALL MY FEELINGS ARE ATTACHED WITH THIS. SELECTION OF VIRTUE AND VICE, I DON'T CARE OF VICE.

I LIVE IN THE DOMESTIC WORLD.

22) BEFORE DOING ANY WORK, I UNDERSTAND ITS PROCESS. THERE IS NOTHING ABOUT VIRTUE AND VICE.

23) NO ONE REMAINS, NO ONE WILL REMAIN. NO ONE CANNOT REMAIN.

THIS WORLD IS A PICTURE, THE IMAGINATION OF A GREAT POET.

24) WHO SAID THAT LIFE WENT IN VAIN.

COME FOR A WHILE AND SIT DOWN NEAR.

YOU WILL REALIZE AND FEEL GOOD.

25) IT IS NOT OBJECT OF IMAGINATION, THOUGHT DOESN'T REMAIN WITHIN LIMIT.

IT'S NOT WORSHIP WITHIN CAPACITY.

THAT IS UNIVERSAL TRUTH.

26) LEARN TO SPEAK THE TRUTH.

IF DEATH COMES TO YOU, YOU WILL BE STRUNG WITH FLOWERS OF IMMORTAL.

27) AFTER CRORES OF REBIRTH A MAN BECOMES GOD.

FOR AGES LIKE OCEAN A MAN HOLDS A MAN WITHIN A WINK.

28) PURITY, THAT IS WHY I WORK HARD.

I WORK HARD FOR THE BENEFIT OF THE MANKIND.

29) THE SONG IS THE BEST WORSHIP.

IT DOESN'T REQUIRE FLOWER, SCENT OF CHANDAN (A PIECE OF HOLY WOOD PASTE) AND CHANTING OF MANTRA/TANTRA (HOLY WORDS).

30) GETTING UP FROM SLEEP AT DAWN YOU PAY HOMAGE TO THE PARENTS, GURU (THE SUPREME MASTER) AND THE SHRINES.

~ SHRI SHRI TAKUR BHABAPAGLA.

31) ON STAYING AT HOME YOU WILL GET HIM, WHY TO TRAVELL IN A FOREST IN VAIN. SIT SILENTLY IN THE CORNER OF THE ROOM, CLOSE YOUR EYES TO SEE (HIM).

32) OH MIND, BE CLEVER, BUT DON'T GET RUINED. YOU MAY BE FAKIR/ MONK NOT MORE THAN THAT. SURRENDER EVERYTHING TO HIM, BUT DON'T SHUN YOUR WORK.

33) THINK, THINK TO KNOW HIM. THEN THERE IS END OF THINKING.

34) DON'T SACRIFICE MALE GOAT, BUFFALO WHICH ARE SONS OF MOTHER OF THE UNIVERSE. SACRIFICE YOUR SIX SENSES OF PASSION (STOIC PASSION, ANGER AND TEMPTATION ETC.) THEN SHYAMA WILL APPEAR.

35) THE BRINDABAN IS NOT VISITED FORCEFULLY, THE BRINDABAN IS VISITED BY JOINING BOTH HANDS.

36) OH MY SON YOU MUST KNOW, LOVE MEANS NOT ONLY LOVE, YOU EXIST IN THE GOODNESS OF A MAN. THAT MEANS YOU MAKE A ROOM OF LOVE IN THE MIND OF THE PEOPLE.

37) MONEY IS PRINTED IN THE MINTS. SUMMONING GOD FROM MENTAL STRENGTH. HE WHO HAS NO MENTAL STRENGTH, HIS LIFE GOES IN VAIN.

38) ALL THINGS ARE AVAILABLE IN EXCHANGE OF MONEY JUST AS GOD IS REALIZED THROUGH DEVOTION.

39) YOU WORSHIP IN AUSPICIOUS MOMENT. WHEN DOES AUSPICIOUS MOMENT COME? WHEN MIND IS DISSOLVED IN THOUGHT.

40) LOVE YOUR COUNTRY. SHUN VIOLENCE, NOT YOUR COUNTRY.

SRI SHRI TAKUR BHABAPAGLA.

41) LEAVE VIOLENCE, LOVE YOUR COUNTRY. YOU EXIST IN THE INNER OF EVERYONE, ONLY THEN YOU WILL VISUALIZE THE VISION OF GOD.

42) MY RELIGION IS TO CONVERT THE WORST INTO THE BEST.

43) HE WHO HAS THE STICK OF JUSTICE, THE STICK OF "YAMA" (GOD OF DEATH) IS AFRAID OF HIM. GOD IS ALSO AFRAID OF HIM.

44) OH MIND, WEIGH YOURSELF CORRECTLY. THEN WEIGH OTHERS. OTHERWISE YOUR SINS ARE NOT FORGIVEN. OH MAN OF NARAYAN (GOD) PAY ATTENTION.

45) ONE WHO FLOATS ON SPRITUAL NAME AND LOVE HAS NO WANT OF LANGUAGE.

46) ONE WHO FEELS HIMSELF SUPERIOR, NO ONE EVER ACCEPTS HIM.

47) ONE WHO WANTS TO FEEL FREE BY SACRIFICING EVERYTHING, ACHIEVES EVERYTHING.

48) A WICKED MAN ESCAPES FOR A MOMENT BUT A PRETENTIOUS MAN CAN NEVER ESCAPE ANYTIME OF THE AGES.

49) YOU CANNOT GET SPRITUAL KNOWLEDGE BY READING BOOKS ONLY. YOU SHOULD LIE DOWN, LIE DOWN ON HIS FEET.

50) GOD DESCENDS FOR THE SINNERS, NOT FOR THE DEVOTEES. LISTEN, ALL THE LIVING BEINGS OF THE WORLD, THE DEVOTEES PRAISE ON CHANTING IN EVERYPLACE AND STALK OF THIS WORLD.

51) TOO MUCH INTELLIGENCE IS NOT GOOD, ONE WHO SPEAKS WITHOUT KNOWING. IT HAPPENS ON WHOM IT WILL HAPPEN AUTOMATICALLY.

52) AFTER IMMERSION, DON'T GET POISON.

53) WHAT IS FAITH? ONE WHO BREATHES EVERY MOMENT BY BREAKING BARRIER OF LOGIC AND DEBATE.

54) IT WILL SUBTRACT THE WORLD AFFAIRS, IT WOULD NOT BE DIFFICULT TO LEARN SACRIFICE FOR YOU.

55) PLENTY OF SINNERS, ONLY ONE GOD EXISTS AND APPEARS IN ALL AGES. THE RAM IN TRETA (2ND AGE) THE SHYAM IN THWAPAR (3RD AGE) THE GOURHARI IN KALI (LAST AGE). THE NAME OF HARI SMELTS THE STONE.

56) THAT YOU ARE LIVING, THIS IS WONDERFUL. THERE IS NO CELIBACY. IF YOU WOULD HAVE A LITTLE PATIENCE, THERE WOULD BE ENDLESS OF WEALTH.

57) REMEMBER, THE SUPREME POWER COVERS THE WHOLE WORLD. DON'T BE DISPLACED. IF YOU FACE BAD INCIDENT, RETAIN RESPECT AND FAITH.

58) THE MESSAGE OF BHABA IS BHABANI.

59) WHATEVER "BHABANI" (GODDESS) WHISPERS INTO THE EARS OF BHABA THAT I REVEAL TO THE DEVOTEE AND DON'T KEEP IT SECRET.

60) THE ANGER OF BHABA IS A LINE ON THE SURFACE OF WATER, I AM ALWAYS HAPPY.

61) BHABA TELLS, "A LITTLE BIT OF GOODNESS IS THE LIGHT OF THE WAY.

62) EVEN DON'T RESPECT BHABA, RESPECT THE MESSAGES, YOU WILL GET SHELTER IN THE LAP OF MOTHER (ALMIGHTY).

63) DEPEND UPON HIM WITHOUT ANY FEAR, YOU WILL SEE THAT THERE IS NO FEAR.

64) SO MANY TECHNIQUES OF BHABA IS MY MOTHER'S (ALMIGHTY) MAGIC.

65) ONE WHO REMAINS IN THOUGHT DOESN'T HAVE ANY CRISIS.

66) WHEN DEATH IS CERTAIN, THEN EMBRACE DEATH LIKE A HERO.

67) ALL ARE EQUAL TO MOTHER (ALMIGHTY) WHETHER THE HINDU OR THE MUSLIM WHOEVER.

68) BEAUTY OF MOTHER (ALMIGHTY) EXISTS EVERYWHER, ONE WHO SEES BECOMES MAD (DIVINE).

69) BONDAGE ARISES IN MIND, SALVATION AND PURITY ALSO ARISE IN MIND.

70) YOU NEED NOT SALUTE TEMPLE TO TEMPLE, IF YOU PROVE YOURSELF ARE GOD. SHRI SHRI TAKUR BHABAPAGLA.

71) (MIND) YOU DID MISTAKE THE SUMMATION LEARN TO MEDITATE/YOG ON THE SEAT OF MEDITATION/YOG. GODDESS OF YOGA/ MEDITATION IS THE ORIGIN OF ALL SUMS.

72) DON'T SPEAK RELEGIOUS WORDS TO THE FOOLS, THEY WILL NEVER LISTEN RATHER THEY WILL FOLLOW THE OPPOSITE.

73) A MAN PASSES AWAY LEAVING BEHIND MEMORY, ONLY A LITTLE MEMORY. LOVING A LOT HE GOES AWAY TO THE UNKNOWN COUNTRY/ PLACE, HE NEVER RETURNS.

74) "KALI"(GODDESS) IS THE EMBODIMENT OF BHABA, THE MIND IS BLACK GOLD (THE GOD KRISHNA) OF BHABA.

75) OH MIND, YOU GO AHEAD, AGAIN DON'T GO BACK. THERE IS SUPREME PLEASURE AHEAD, THERE IS PRETENC AT THE BACKWARD.

76) A MAN BECOMES GOD AND THE INCARNATION. BHABA TELLS, EXTEEND YOUR VISION.

77) A MAN IS THE GREATEST GOD. LOVE AND GET CLOSE TO THE PEOPLE, THEN ONLY THERE WILL BE GREAT UNION.

78) DON'T REST YOUR MIND ENGAGE YOURSELF TO PRAY AT HIS FEET.

79) DEATH LISTENS TO NONE. IT MAY APPEAR ALWAYS, ANYTIME, ANYWHERE AND ANY MOMENT.

80) LOOKING THROUGH THE MIND LEADS TO THE TRUTH, LOOKING THROUGH THE EYES IS UNREAL SHRI SHRI TAKUR BHABAPAGLA.

81) IT IS DIFFICULT TO KNOW THE PEOPLE OF THIS WORLD.

WHEN YOU WILL COME TO KNOW THE PEOPLE THEN YOU WILL BE ACQUAINTED WITH THIS WORLD.

82) A MAN IS A GOD, PAY RESPECT, DON'T INSULT HIM.

83) AS LONG AS YOU EXIST, HE EXISTS. IF HE DOESN'T EXIST, YOU DON'T EXIST.

84) HE WHO TOLERATES WILL REMAIN. HE WHO DOESN'T TOLERATE WILL PERISH.

85) THOSE WHO OBSERVE GOD IN EVERY LIVING BEING ARE ALMIGHTY GOD.

86) WHEN THE LIGHT WILL GO OFF, THE WORLD WILL BE COVERED WITH DARKNESS.

THEN WHO WILL BE THE SUPREME MASTER, WHO IS TO BE DISCIPLE IN THIS WORLD?

87) HE WHO UTTERS THE NAME OF HIM/ HER IN THE MORNING AND EVENING WILL NEVER DIE.

HE BECOMES IMMORTAL AND LIES DOWN AT HIS/ HER ILLUMINATED FEET.

88) MORE YOU WILL SEARCH THE CHANDI, THE GEETA BOOK YOU WILL GET LOST.

89) SELF DEPENDENT IS GOD, SEE TO OPEN THE BOOK OF YOUR MIND.

90) HE WHO RESPONDS TO EVERY ONE'S MIND, OBSERVES THE EXISTENCE OF YOGA MAYA (GODDESS)

91) WHOM I INVOKE AND GET RESPONSE, HE IS MY DEAREST.

92) WHOM YOU HOLD, HE IS GREAT. WHY DO YOU DIE HOLDING THIS AND THAT?

93) IF YOU CAN HOW TO WRITE, ALL INKS ARE GOOD.

94) DON'T BE AFRAID OF DEATH TO SUBDUE THE ENEMY.

95) IT CANNOT BE SEEN WITH VACANT EYES, IT SHOULD BE SEEN THROUGH THE MIND.

96) WHY DO THE SAINTS COVER THEIR BODIES WITH ASH ? BHABA TELLS, "IF YOU COVER THE BODY WITH ASH, IT WILL GET SPREAD IN THE WORLD.

97) CONSUME EVERYTHING BUT DON'T CONSUME YOUR BRAIN.

98) THE STRAIGHT PATH INDICATES COMPLETE SURRENDER.

99) SELF CONTROL MEANS TO MAINTAIN UNIFORMITY, RESTRAINT AND RULE. THIS IS THE WORD OF THE SCRIPTURE.

100) WHAT IS SIMPLICITY ? WHOSE MIND DOESN'T DEGRADED BY MEANS OF TRICK, FORCE AND PRETENCE.

101) LEADING THE DOMESTIC LIFE IF YOU GET SOMETIME, PRAY TO GOD. BHABA TELLS.

102) WHEN THE WHITE PAPER IS CREASED, A PICTURE CANNOT BE DRAWN. THEN THE PICTURE OF CHITRANI (SELF PICTURE) IS NOT EXPOSED WITHOUT MAINTAINING ONE'S CHARACTER.

103) WORSHIP WITH THE MUSIC AND SONGS, YOU WILL GET STRENGTH IN YOUR MIND. THE SPIRITUAL STRENGTH OF GODDESS WILL BE SEATED IN YOUR HEART.

104) WHO IS NONVIOLENT MAN? AS A DOOR WITHOUT RIVET.

105) TO PERCEIVE GOD DOESN'T REQUIRE MONEY, REQUIRES PRAYER.

106) HOW DOES A MIND SETTLE ? BY TURNING THE MIND (MANA) UPSIDE DOWN TO PRAY (NAMA).

107) ONE WHO HAS A NARROW MIND GETS AFRAID AT THE SLIGHTEST.

THOSE WHO ARE SONS OF ABHAYA (THE GODDESS WHO BESTOWS COURAGE) ARE NOT AFRAID OF ANYONE.

108) EVERYONE HAS TO FALL ASLEEP AT THE END OF LIFE, DON'T BE PROUD. REGENT OF DEATH SMILES TO SEE YOU.

109) DEPEND UPON HIM, WHO REMAINS IN EVERYONE'S HEART.

110) WHICH PLANT'S LEAF IS BEAUTYFULL? SIMPLICITY AS A LEAF. SHRI SHRI TAKUR BHABAPAGLA.

111) WITHOUT CONCENTRATION NOBODY REALIZES GOD.

112) IF YOU DON'T PERFORM "DUTY", "BEAUTY" IS NOT ENHANCED. WHEN" "BEAUTY" IS ENHANCED," "MAA BETI" (GODDESS) BECOMES MERCIFUL.

113) SHUN VIOLENCE, LOVE YOUR COUNTRY. IF YOU EXIST IN EVERYONE 'S HEART , YOU WILL OBSERVE GOD.

114) EXPLAIN IN BRIEF, IS IT RIGHT ? A) DON'T RELY ON THE FUTURE. B) FORGET THE PAST. C) LOVE THE PRESENT.

115) OH MIND YOU LEARN :-- WHAT IS SIMPLICITY ? WHOSE MIND IS NOT CHANGEABLE BY VIRTUE OF TRICK, FORCE AND PRETENCE.

WHAT IS TRUTH? THINKING ABOUT MORTALITY, WHO PASSES SMILING EVERY DAY.

WHAT IS FAITH ? BREAKING BARRIER OF LOGIC AND DEBATE WHO BREATHES EVERY MOMENT.

WHAT IS DEVOTION? TO SURRENDER SELF WITHOUT DESIRE.

116) "THE CONSISTENCY" OF "THE NATURE". I HAVE NO SYMPATHY. I HAVE DUTY. I HAVE NO RETIREMENT. I HAVE WORK. I HAVE NONE. I HAVE MYSELF.

117) IF WATER FALLS IN MUD, FLOWER OF LOVE BLOOMS.

118) BE HAPPY , ENJOY, DO YOUR DUTY.

119) THOSE WHO REALIZE GOD IN EVERY LIVING BEING ARE GOD.

120) SURRENDER TO HIM IN ALL RESPECT. HE WILL SERVE YOU EVERYTHING LIKE A SERVANT. SHRI SHRI TAKUR BHABAPAGLA.

121) MOMENT AFTER MOMENT, UTTER AND UTTER THE NAME OF KRISHNA, THE NAME OF KRISHNA, THE NAME OF KRISHNA.

122) THOSE WHO DON'T CARE OF TOUCHABILITY AND UNTOUCHABILITY ARE BEAUTIFUL "GOURANGA" (GOD) OF BHABA.

123) WORSHIP CANNOT BE ACCOMPLISHED WITH WEAKNESS. ROUSE THE LIFE OF EVERYONE, ESTABLISH, YOU TOO ARE GOOD, THIS IS FIRM IMAGINATION.

124) REMEMBER, NO ONE WILL REMAIN IN THIS WORLD. DON'T TAKE CARE OF SELF INTEREST.

125) DON'T USE UNPLEASANT WORD TO YOUR NEAR AND DEAR ONES. DON'T SAY BAD, NOT--SO-- DEAR EXCEPT GOOD WORD.

126) BE HONEST IN THE DOMESTIC LIFE. SPEAK SWEET AND SMILE.

PICK UP GOOD THINGS, DON'T SEE FAULT OF OTHERS.

127) THE EXISTENCE IS FALSE, MORTALITY IS TRUTH.

YOU ARE DISSOLVED IN THE UNTRUTH AND WORTHLESS AFFAIRS.

128). REMEMBER A LITTLE ABOUT CONSCIENCE AND SACRIFICE, IT WILL PERFORM IN THE LAST MOMENT.

129) IT'S BREATHING WITHOUT BELIEF THAT'S WHY I ORDER THE MIND TO SPEAK THE NAME OF KALI. WHEN IT WILL EMTY IN DECEIT FORGETTING ILLUSION OF THE BODY.

130) OH MIND, YOU HAVE LEARNT MANY THINGS, HAVE YOU EVER LEARNT TO LOVE EVERYONE?.

132) I WILL CALL HIM A "MAN" WHO LOVES YOU AND ME EUALLY.

133) THE PATH OF WORSHIP IS FILLED WITH THORNS, WHICH SHOULD BE TRAVELED ATTENTIVELY. KEEP ON UTTERING THE GREAT NAME (GOD) WHILE PASSING THROUH THE ZIG ZAG PATH.

134) DON'T PRAISE THE COMPLXION, PRAISE THE QUALITY OF A MAN. THE ROTTEN BODY WILL TARNISH, WHO WILL REMAIN IN THIS WORLD?

135) TO RESPECT THE SPIRITUAL MASTER IS NOT AN EASY TASK. IF YOU DISTRUST THE MASTER, IT WILL LEAD YOU TO HELL.

136) HOW WILL YOU WORSHIP? HOLD, KILL, CUT, EAT.

HOLD--- HOLD GOD. TAKE MOTHER'S (GODDESS) NAME.

KILL---- TO ABSTAIN FROM SELF APPRECIATION AND SUBDUE ANIMALITY.

CUT---- TO SUPPRESS ILLUSIONARY AFFAIRS.

EAT--- TO INTAKE NECTAR OF LOVE.

137) AT FIRST CONQUER THE ABILITY TO FORGIVE

138) WHAT EVER YOU WANT, MOTHER (GODDESS) HAS ALL THE WAYS.

139) ONE WHO KNOWS THE SPIRITUAL MASTER IS GREATER THAN "KRISHNA" AND IS A AN AFFECTIONATE MAN. THEY KNOW THE DESTINATION.

140) OH MOTHER (GODDESS) PROVIDE ME STRENGTH TO MY ARMS AND DEVOTION IN MY HEART.

141) THE ORNAMENT OF FOUR AGES. IN 1ST ERA / SATYA YUGA -- SWEET WORD.

IN 2ND ERA/ TRETA YUGA -- DOUBT

IN 3RD ERA/ THWAPARA YUGA -- HIDE AND SEEK. IN LAST ERA/ KOLI YUGA --- VIOLENCE.

142) JABA BHABA WORSHIPS TO MOTHER (GODDESS) DAILY BEFORE EVERYONE.

143) "AAMAKAY" (ME) REMOVE AA, IT BECOMES MAKAY (MOTHER GODDESS)." TAMAKAY" (YOU), REMOVE TA, IT BECOMES MAKAY. EVERYONE IS PART OF MOTHER (GODDESS).

144) DON'T RELY ON BREATHING, THAT'S WHY I CALL UPON THE MIND TO CHANT THE NAME OF KALI (GODDESSES).

145) WHERE DOES GOD EXIST? EVERYWHERE.

146) THE WATER, FOREST AND THE OWNER ARE NOT TO BE TRUSTED.

IN WATER DIFFERENT TYPES OF CREATURES LIVE.

IN THE FOREST THE TIGER LIVES.

THE OWNER FOR WHOM YOU SERVE AT HOME, THAT GREAT MASTER CAN BANISH YOU AT ANY MOMENT.

147) I CRY AND LAUGH AS MUCH AS I CAN. THEY ARE MY BEST FRIENDS, I AM THEIR SLAVE.

148) "KALI" (GODDESS) IS THE EMBODIMENT OF BHABA, THE MIND IS THE BLACK GOLD (LORD KRISHNA).

149) OH MIND, YOU HAVE LEARNT MANY THINGS. HAVE YOU LEARNT TO LOVE EVERYONE?

150) GOD IS NONE, A MAN IS A GOD. DON'T NEGLECT, GIVE RESPECT TO HIM.

Preface

In September 1970, burdened with the plight of my father battling paralysis, I embarked on a journey to Kalna, to the revered Ashram of Bhaba Pagla. It was here, during the grandeur of Durga Puja, that the profound encounter unfolded. The first meeting with Bhaba Pagla, marked by his gentle smile and genuine inquiries, left an enduring impression, offering a glimpse of his caring and compassionate nature. This captivating demeanour drew me back each month, seeking the blessings and guidance of Bhaba Pagla, a source of solace and hope during our family's trials.

My relationship with Bhaba Pagla was marked by spiritual guidance that transcended the physical constraints of my father's paralysis. Bhaba Pagla's instructions to place Java flowers under my father's bed and the recommendation of chanting the Gayatri mantra instilled profound hope in our hearts. The grim tragedy of my father's passing in July 1971 brought forth moments of divine grace.

One significant day, I was immersed in the divine energy as Bhaba Pagla and Pagli Ma stood side by side. Torn about whose feet to touch first, I approached Bhaba Pagla, allowing the profound influence of his energy to shape my intellect. This spiritual guidance became the catalyst leading to my successful clearing of the Indian Institute of Metals exam in 1979.

Despite setbacks caused by negative influences, my mother sought Bhaba Pagla's divine intervention, which transformed my understanding and reinforced my unyielding resolve to seek his blessings. Miraculously, Bhaba Pagla's divine assurance ushered my qualification in a medical test, even while wearing myopia glasses.

These deeply transformative experiences affirm the profound truth in Bhaba Pagla's words, shaping my faith and guiding my life's journey, where personal encounters become testament to the enduring legacy of spiritual guidance and unity.

The inspiration to write this book stems from the profound impact of these encounters with Bhaba Pagla, where his spiritual guidance transformed my perspective and defined the course of my life. The book aims to weave the experiences of many with Bhaba Pagla into the broader narrative of his journey, showcasing the transformative impact of spiritual leadership amidst historical challenges that unfolded against the backdrop of profound personal encounters, intertwining enduring spiritual guidance and overall with the transformative impact on me.

I have strived to capture the profound truth of spiritual guidance and unity delivered through the eternal power of Bhaba Pagla, shaping the narrative as a testament to the timeless influence of spiritual guidance and the enduring legacy of unity.

Foreword

JOY BHABA
Founded by Bhabapagla

BHABAR MAHASHAKTIR ASHRAY

(A Public Charitable Trust)
P. O. : SUKCHAR, KOLKATA - 700 115
Mob : 93398 42442, 94326 69084, (033) 2553 5412

I, Shri Someshwananda Giri would observe Niramay Khasnobis in the Ashram (Hermitage) of Bhaba Pagla in the Kalna Temple of Maa Bhabami under the district of Bardhaman situated in West Bengal whenever he used to arrive at Kalna temple.

We would address him as Babul Da name whenever he encountered us to inquire.

His simplicity and sweetness would captivate me.

I discussed many miraculous incidents of Bhaba Pagla with him.

He selected the miraculous incidents of Bhaba Pagla from the Book,Param Guru Bhaba Pagla written by Tomonash Bandopadhyay,a renowned professor.

I wish him all success to endeavour for propagating the miraculous incidents of Bhaba Pagla in this book named Miraculous saint of India,Bhaba Pagla.

Today,on this day
26th Jan,2024.

With blessings of Bhaba Pagla,
Thanking You,

SWAMI SOMESHWANANDA GIRI
COUNCILLOR OF BHABA PAGLA

The Great Festival of Dol Jatra, Holi Festival (Full-moon-day for coloured festival-play) of Lord Shri Shri Krishna is an auspicious day. Inauguration of this holy book is preferred on this day, Monday, 25" March, 2024 (5th Chaitra, 1430 Bangabda as per Bengali Calendar) Celebrated at Bhabar Mahashaktir Ashray, (Hermitage) Sukchar, Kolkata-700115.

Contents

CHAPTER 1

Birth & Early Life

In the verdant landscapes of East Bengal, nestled within the tranquil village of Amta, part of the Manikgunge Subdivision in the district of Dhaka, was born an individual who would later be venerated as the miraculous saint, *Bhaba Pagla*. This revered locality, now a part of Bangladesh, was home to the illustrious and affluent Saha Chaudhury lineage, into which *Bhaba Pagla* was born.

His earthly presence was ushered in by his father, Gajendra Mohan, and his mother, Gayasundari Devi—a woman of remarkable simplicity and devout piety. Their household was already blessed with children; the eldest son, Girindra Mohan, was a renowned *Vaishnav* saint who resided in Kolkata, his reputation cemented not only by his spiritual eminence but also his prosperous jute trading endeavours.

Following *Girindra Mohan* were three daughters, each bestowing their own unique radiance upon the family: Kiran Sashi, Nani Bala, and Tapu. Yet destiny held further plans for Gayasundari Devi as she was to bring forth two additional souls into the world, the twin brothers *Debendra Mohan* and *Bhabendra Mohan*. It was *Bhabendra Mohan*, later known as *Bhaba Pagla*, who graced this world mere moments after his twin.

Amidst the joy of impending new life, tension gripped the family when, at five months' gestation, Gayasundari Devi's health alarmingly declined. It was at this juncture that Dr. U N Bramhachari, an esteemed physician celebrated for his pioneering work in the development of a treatment for black fever, was called upon to assess her condition. His expert diagnosis was grim; Gayasundari *Devi* was in dire straits. Upon careful examination using his stethoscope, the doctor anticipated he would encounter the sombre silence of a dire situation within the womb. Instead, to his utter astonishment, he discerned the delightful sound of one of the infants' laughter. This unexpected moment left Dr. Bramhachari befuddled and filled with wonder.

With the pregnancy precarious and the mother's life in jeopardy, a decision loomed over them, fraught with the perilous choice between the well-being of the mother and her unborn children. Then, in an unforeseen turn, with no prior warning, Gayasundari Devi experienced a sharp, sudden pain. She collapsed to the floor, losing consciousness, her fate and that of her twins hanging by a thread.

What followed could only be described as a stroke of the miraculous—a phenomenon that defied the apprehensions of those who stood vigil. Against all odds, life found its way through the darkness of uncertainty, cementing the narrative of *Bhaba Pagla's* extraordinary arrival into this world—an arrival marked by mystery and the touch of the divine.

On the day in question, an assistant witnessed something remarkable: A large baby was born, and astonishingly, the newborn spoke, telling its mother, "I will come back soon, 'ma', you will not suffer anymore."

The assistant, taken aback and scarcely believing her own ears, was nonetheless swift to react, preserving a stone bowl stained with blood, which can still be found in the Ma *Bhaba*ni temple in Kalna.

Following this mysterious vanishment, the baby's family and mother were enveloped in a sense of dreamy anticipation, waiting for the day of maturity.

Ultimately, the birth occurred on an auspicious evening known as Koja Gori Lakshmi Poornima, which is the full moon dedicated to Goddess Lakshmi. It happened after 8:45 pm on a Friday in the month of Ashwin, marking a lunar eclipse. Through evaluating peer ages and astronomical calculations, this date was determined to be the 31st of Ashwin, 1309 Bongabda—a night of a lunar eclipse—which corresponds to Friday, October 17th, 1902, as per English calendar. The last daughter born was named Satiaagmoni.

The genealogy list was compiled by Girindra Mohan Chaudhary, with the acknowledgment directed to his third son, Gadadhar Chaudhary. These details were derived from a book entitled "Param Guru Baba *Pagla*," authored by the esteemed professor Tamonash Bandopadhyay.

Notably, many incarnations of deities such as Buddha, Guru Nanak, and Gouranga Maha Prabhu, among other revered personalities, are believed to have been born on full moon days.

The narrative of the magnificent Jesus Christ begins in Bethlehem, within the metropolis of Jerusalem. His mother, Saint Mary or the Blessed Virgin Mary, and his father, Saint Joseph, are central figures.

One gospel recount how Mary, traversing a desert path, succumbed to a desert storm, collapsing as a searing gust and a spark entered her being. It was at this time Joseph had a vision that Jesus, as God, was imminent. Sheltered by Joseph in a stable, Mary gave birth there amidst divine omens.

At Jesus' birth, seven stars appeared in the sky. Five wise men, or Magis, travelled from India to Jerusalem, guided by these stars to the holy site.

Another divine birth story involves Sri Ramakrishna. His father, Kshudiram Chattopadhyay, experienced a revelatory dream at the Gaya shrine during rites dedicated to his late father. Narayan

(God) acclaimed Kshudiram's devotion in the dream, promising to be born to him. Ramakrishna's mother, Chandra Moni Devi, was at the Lord Shiva temple offering her prayers when a severe hailstorm and thunderbolt broke out. It was during this chaos that she sensed a bright luminescence enter her—as if someone had found refuge within her womb.

Then there is another miraculous narrative concerning Ma Sarda, the divine consort of Ramakrishna Paramahansa Dev. Ma Sarda was the daughter of Ramachandra Mukhopadhyay and Shyama Sundari Devi. As the story goes, Shyama Sundari Devi was walking beneath a stone apple tree when she witnessed a radiant young girl with fair skin, in a red and scarlet gown, descending from the tree. When this girl embraced Shyama Sundari Devi, she exclaimed, "Oh Ma, I have come to you." Overwhelmed by a sudden burst of light, Shyama Sundari Devi lost consciousness, and it is told that at that moment, a divine presence entered her being. Over time, she would become the mother of an extraordinary divine lady.

The biographer of Guru Nanak wrote that the village erupted in loud laughter at the moment of his birth. The entire village was eager to glimpse the infant, already sensing the divine nature of the child's future.

The young life of *Bhaba Pagla,* born *Bhaben*dra, was marked by exceptional displays of spirituality. As the younger of twin brothers, his devotion to God drew the admiration of all those around him. From a young age, he worshiped the Divine Mother and engaged in profound conversations.

One day, at the age of five, *Bhaben*dra's father, Gajendra, playfully suggested that his son's temperament would suit the role of a police officer. Sitting in his father's lap, *Bhabendra* inquired with curiosity:

*Bhaben*dra: "Father, what kind of man is a police officer?"

Father: "A policeman is someone who maintains order. They serve the state, especially during this British rule."

*Bhaben*dra: "But Father, is there not someone above them?"

Gajendra, struck by the depth of his son's question, replied: "Yes, my son. There is Mother Jagadamba, the Divine Mother, who is greater than any worldly ruler."

The villagers soon came to recognize *Bhabendra* as a divine child, as his childhood was filled with miraculous events.

He crafted a statue of the Mother Kali from clay and adorned it with colours. This sacred statue was placed beneath a Gab (Diospyros Malabarica) tree, in the southwest corner of the house, where *Bhabendra* would worship. This tree became the sanctified site for the worship of Mother Kali.

Bhabendra introduced the tradition of creating sweets from clay, like Sandesh cakes, and during the worship, would cover the clay offerings with a white cloth. Miraculously, at the end of the rituals, these clay sweets would transform into real confections.

The children proclaimed their joy at the authentic taste of the sweets, and even the adults, upon hearing the children's excitement, tasted and confirmed the transformation of the clay sweets into genuine delights.

On being asked how it was possible, *Bhabendra* explained that the process of transformation required just one secret ingredient—that when added to anything, it could effect change.

He playfully suggested that "if you add one to one, it becomes two, showing how adding something could bring about transformation." His clever riddles and acts spread his reputation throughout the village. Such experiences with the divine were commonly shared under the Gab tree.

At night, *Bhabendra* would lose himself in meditation and worship of the Divine Mother. His dedication was so intense that even offerings of clay were said to be transformed into milk and curds by his contemplative power.

Years later, Tamonash Bandyopadhyay, an author, inquired about these extraordinary happenings from *Bhaba Pagla,* who affirmed that many more wondrous things occurred that defied simple explanation.

Bhaba Pagla, a revered saint in India, often conveyed his profound spiritual insights through simple yet symbolic acts. He would cover the offerings to the Goddess Kali with a white cloth and claim that, with childlike innocence, the Mother Almighty would bless the offerings with her touch. He believed that to see the hand of the Divine Mother would strike fear into the hearts of his friends due to its sacred nature.

At the tender age of five or six, *Bhaba Pagla* composed songs that expressed his deep spiritual longings. One such song pleaded with the Goddess Tara to ease the pain in his heart. His devotion was such that he composed a thousand songs in her honour, distributing wisdom and devotion as if they were nectar. People from his village, Amta, bore witness to his extraordinary abilities.

The songs suggested *Bhaba Pagla's* soul had journeyed through various epochs: the Satya Yuga (Golden Age), Treta Yuga (Silver Age), Dvapara Yuga (Copper Age), and Kali Yuga (Iron Age). He insinuated that he had been reborn throughout these ages, hinting at his extraordinary nature by telling his mother that any being who can speak immediately after birth cannot be merely human.

Bhaba Pagla grew up alongside his twin brothers, *Bhabendra* Mohan and Devendra Mohan, playing under a Gab tree, known for its velvet apples. While their father, Gajendra Mohan, pondered their education, both twins were admitted to a village school lovingly referred to as "Minor School." *Bhaba Pagla* did not resist this change; he thrived in this new environment and promptly won the admiration of teachers and students alike.

Despite his spiritual pursuits, *Bhaba Pagla* excelled academically, quickly learning. However, when *Bhaba Pagla* faced an unexpected setback, failing an arithmetic test in third grade, he found a deeper meaning in his failure. For him, "Anko," the Bengali word for arithmetic that also means "lap," hinted at a struggle to "climb into the lap of the Mother Goddess."

This failure inspired him to compose a spiritual song about arithmetic and yoga, intertwining them metaphorically to illustrate a journey of self-improvement and enlightenment. The song speaks of using yoga or 'addition' to attain spiritual knowledge and of 'subtraction' to shed worldly desires. He further encourages blooming 'multiplication' of positive attributes and finding joy in the colours.

Through this creative reimagining of mathematical concepts, *Bhaba Pagla* teaches that true understanding lies in embracing the Divine Mother's wisdom, where the arithmetic of life finds its purest expression.

Yogeshwari, the Goddess, is the spiritual foundation of arithmetic, which is also referred to as 'Anka', a term that intriguingly means 'lap' as well. This sacred discipline is said to diminish worldly desires, simplifying the concept of subtraction so that it becomes as enjoyable as counting with warmth and care. As one masters subtraction, the path to understanding multiplication unfolds, and this skill becomes an inherent part of one's knowledge. In mastering division, one experiences satisfaction akin to the fair judgment found in the courts of law. However, it is often not the fortunate but the fool who grapples with 'Anka'—the arithmetic—in a confused manner.

Bhaba Pagla contemplates which mathematical operations—addition, subtraction, multiplication, and division—he should apply within the greater framework of the divine 'Mother's Arithmetic'. By forgoing all worldly attachments, he strives to create a perfect calculation in this sacred version of arithmetic, seeking an error-free result in the haven of 'Anka', the mother's lap. To saints and sages, the lap of the mother, or the Goddess's embrace, is a sanctuary for devotion.

In the rural setting of Bhakuliya, which lies adjacent to Aamta Village, the young *Bhabendra* spent his days. The Chowhat River flows nearby, its waters a tributary of the majestic Dhaleshwari River. From his home, *Bhabendra* would make the one-and-a-half-mile journey to the crematorium in Bhakuliya. The crematorium, a site where life meets its earthly end, became a place of deep reflection and spiritual discovery for the young seeker.

In the silence of the empty crematorium, *Bhabendra* would often sing about Shyama, the Goddess, picturing her dance to conquer foes. His melodies were too profound for Bidhubhushan to fully grasp.

In another hymn, *Bhaba Pagla* sang with heartfelt emotion: "My Mother is Dakshina Kali. I share with Her my stories of sorrow and joy." Again, his voice would swell with reverence as he sang: "Mother, what kind of laughter is yours? Such a laugh, Mother; it's a playful act of yours, even without creation. The crematorium, it is your home."

Bhabendra would while away the hours, deeply immersed in singing about the diverse aspects of the Almighty Mother, sometimes as Shashan Kali, the deity of the crematorium, and other times as Dakshina Kali, another manifestation of Goddess Kali.

He would gaze intently into the vast emptiness of the sky, as if locking eyes with an unseen presence. Bidhubhushan watched, both amazed and mystified by *Bhaben*'s behavior, sharing these accounts with friends who in turn became engrossed in discussions about *Bhaben*. His activities stirred a mix of curiosity and concern in those around him, particularly his anxious parents, who noticed his preference for the crematorium over school or worship under the Gab tree.

Friends posed the question, "Why do you frequent the crematorium?"

To which *Bhaben* replied crisply, "To sharpen (shaan) oneself in the crematorium."

Perplexed, they further inquired the meaning. "To sharpen oneself is to hone intelligence and clear away muddled thoughts," *Bhaben* clarified.

The common folk failed to perceive that *Bhaben* had delved into a spiritual realm—a place where even seasoned spiritual worshippers hesitated, some halted by visions of ghosts, while others became conceited, believing to possess 'Ashta Siddhi', or the 'Power of Fulfilling Eight Desires'.

It was in the crematorium that *Bhaben*dra, greeted by spectres, heard the serene and familiar voice that had accompanied him since childhood, the voice of Abhaya, the Goddess, saying, "Why do you fear? I am with you." This soft assurance granted him the courage to remain fearless amidst the solitary haunting visions by the river's bank.

The following day, equipped with a sketchbook and pen, *Bhaben* returned to the crematorium. There, he was visited by a series of phantasmal images, each one appearing in turn. With pen in hand, he meticulously crafted their likenesses, transcribing thirty-two different spectres onto paper. The caring gaze of the Almighty Mother watched over him, and she inquired about the names of each image as *Bhaben* completed their sketches.

This sketchbook, a testament to his spiritual encounters, is still preserved today in the 'Maa *Bhaba*ni' temple at Kalna. The haunting figures that *Bhaben* sketched were later given names, which have been documented in the book *'Param Guru Bhaba Pagla'* by the distinguished professor Tamonash Bandhopadhyay.

The names he recorded for the male entities are the following:

1)Hilli, 2) Milli, 3) Killi, 4) Billi, 5) Chilli, 6) Khilli, 7) Lilli, 8) Hakka, 9) Mugli, 10) Hissa, 11) Chumba, 12) Tircha, 13) Ningsi, 14) Skandha Kata, 15) Pitil (The Circling Wind), and 16) Muksa.

And for the female entities, their names are listed as:

1) Jangi, 2) Mirki, 3) Baishal, 4) Chharmaghura (One Who Jumps), 5) Bismalong, 6) Kurtabaaz, 7) Shakunkila, 8) Bragha Bali, 9) Basansa, 10) Turki, 11) Lombasha (Jhalkan), 12) Burkaghai, 13) Jukta Gaandha (Bodyguard of the Mother, who remains near Her), 14) Botal, 15) Sankramak, and 16) Ashanti.

Hilli, and Skandhakata and Baishal emerged as leaders of the male and female groups, respectively, with Jukta Gaandha also a prominent figure among the latter. Each group consisted of seven companions; in total, four groups with twenty-eight companions. Including the leaders, there were thirty-two ghostly spirits.

These spirits played the roles of messengers and junior messengers for other, more potent spirits in service to the Almighty Mother. As *Bhaben* chanted the sacred words devoted to the mother, he was able to pacify these extraordinary apparitions instantly.

Bhaba Pagla's heart was filled with immeasurable joy due to the compassionate nature of the Almighty Mother. Consequently, thirty-two disciples of the Divine Mother grew to become close companions and were humbled before *Bhaba Pagla* by the grace of the great and merciful Mother.

Days later, another miraculous event took place—it was a vision of sublime grace, a rarity amidst the many beautiful experiences. This occurrence was unmatched in its significance, save perhaps for Bhabha *Pagla* himself. The Almighty Mother's love has been manifesting through such divine events for eons, each one exceptional and unparalleled. On this occasion, the Almighty Mother spoke, inviting *Bhaba* to observe: "Look at me. On my forehead sits an unwavering eye without lashes, open eternally." She offered herself as a subject for his artistic depiction. "Draw me. Capture my image now as I sit before you." She then positioned herself with majestic poise.

With careful strokes of his paintbrush, *Bhaben* captured her likeness to perfection. The image he created was none other than that of the Almighty Mother of the Universe, a session that spanned approximately two and a half hours. It was a profound moment as the Almighty Mother remained seated for the duration, allowing *Bhaben* to complete his masterpiece.

This precious artwork, a portrait of the Divine Mother, is safeguarded to this day. Ensconced within the sacred space of the 'Maa *Bhaba*ni' temple at Kalna, it is veiled respectfully by a cloth, continuing to be a cherished relic of spiritual wonder.

Bhaba Pagla's profound spiritual insights and miraculous abilities have often been compared to the great philosopher Shankaracharya, who was renowned for his vast knowledge and spiritual powers. However, his mother, Gayasundari Devi, was alarmed by her son's unusual behaviour. Concerned, she brought the matter to the attention of her eldest son, Girindra Mohan, questioning how he could remain silent about *Bhaben*'s habit of visiting the crematorium.

Girindra Mohan proposed a solution to shift *Bhaben* to Kolkata, hoping a change in environment would refocus his younger brother's mind. The family, including their father Gajendra Mohan, agreed to this plan. The news quickly spread through their village, sparking conversations about *Bhaben*, whose otherworldly actions and deep religiosity were beyond the villagers' understanding.

In their village, *Bhaben* was known for his habit of loitering by the riverbank, where women would gather water in clay pitchers. At times, he mischievously tossed stones, breaking their fragile containers. With each pitcher costing between four to six Annas, and sixteen Annas making a Rupee, the financial strain was significant for these poor women. In their frustration, they appealed to Gayasundari Devi for intervention. When confronted by his mother about his behaviour and its impact on the impoverished women, *Bhaben* argued that they should instead be given the brass pitchers from their home. Eventually, his mother acquiesced, gifting the women brass pitchers to replace those *Bhaben* had broken. Looking on with a gentle smile, *Bhaben* noted to his mother how his actions had inadvertently benefited the women.

Word of the plan to send *Bhaben* to Kolkata spread throughout the village, triggering widespread discussion. *Bhaben* was considered an enigma; he seemed to possess an otherworldly knowledge and exhibited spiritual phenomena that many found baffling.

Later, *Bhaben* and his brother Deben arrived at Girindra Mohan's Kolkata residence, where they met with warm hospitality. The friendly gatekeeper fondly likened them to the legendary brothers Ram and Lakshman and even memorized some of their devotional songs.

With their sister-in-law, Radha Kundu, present, the boys settled in comfortably and were enrolled at the nearby Aryan school, not far from the affluent Kundu family's palace. Unlike Deben, who was studious and focused, *Bhaben* remained unchanged by the new surroundings. He was more inclined to compose devotional songs—a trait of his that even touched the school's Bihari gatekeeper, who came to cherish the hymns of *Bhaben* and Deben, becoming their devoted follower.

Ironically, *Bhaba Pagla* often remarked that Jogesh Babu, the headmaster known for using tobacco rolled in Paan leaf, would occasionally discipline the students quite harshly during classes.

****

CHAPTER 2

Bhaba Pagla with His Mother returned to their village

After the passing of their father in Puri Dham, where he breathed his last at the holy site of Swargadwar, Gayasundari Devi and her twelve-year-old twin sons, Deben and *Bhaben*, faced the aftermath with a heavy heart. Deben and *Bhaben* performed the 'Shradha' rites with proper ceremony, guided by their eldest brother, Girindra Mohan, who had also decided to take up the responsibility of their education.

At a poignant moment before this, while mourning by the Ganga River after her husband's death, Gayasundari Devi had an extraordinary experience. She found a stone of the Shalagram, revered as an embodiment of Lord Narayan, miraculously floating on the water's surface. Her son *Bhaba Pagla* recognized it as such and was moved to tears. Gayasundari, interpreting this as a divine sign, embraced the stone, which would later be considered a source of solace and strength during challenging times.

The responsibility for managing the family's land and property fell to Gayasundari Devi, who, along with her sons, eventually made the decision to return to their village after completing the necessary duties in Kolkata.

Recognizing the importance of a sturdy education, Girindra Mohan arranged for Deben and *Bhaben* to be admitted into a boarding school. The chosen institution was the prestigious Brindaban Chandra English High School in Pakutia Village, a few miles from their home in Aamta. This school, established through the endowment of Zamindar Upendra Mandal, had gained a reputation for its high entrance examination standards, which rivalled those of Kolkata schools, and employed brilliant teachers.

During their time at Pakutia B.C. High School, Deben and *Bhaben* were contemporaries of Manindra Mohan Saha, who later recounted their school experiences. However, after reaching class VI, *Bhaba Pagla*, referred to as '*Bhaben* Dada', stopped attending school. This marked the end of his formal primary education.

Manindra Mohan Saha, two grades junior to Deben and *Bhaben* (*Bhaba Pagla*), struggled with arithmetic. Deben, compassionate and helpful, would assist Manindra in improving his mathematical skills. Meanwhile, *Bhaben*'s time was devoted to crafting a statue of the goddess Kali and diligently worshipping her with complete devotion.

Despite being enrolled in the boarding school due to their eldest brother Girindra Mohan's forceful decision, *Bhaben* felt the pull of his spiritual commitments. *Bhaben* often left the boarding school without notice to worship 'Maa Kali' at home, sometimes for eight to ten days, occasionally extending up to fifteen. His absences were met with understanding rather than anger from his teachers, who tried to gently counsel him against such disappearances.

Deben and *Bhaben* were known for their musical talent. They would enchant the school with their soulful renditions of songs dedicated to 'Maa Kali' and Lord Krishna. Their skill with musical instruments — such as the flute, violin, esraj, and harmonium — was remarkable and earned *Bhaben* a gold medal for his proficiency.

An educator at the boarding school, Shree Chandra Babu, would often sing 'Pathabali' (ancient songs of Radha-Krishna) with *Bhaben*. In these performances, *Bhaben* would immerse the audience with his devotional music, celebrating both the Divine Mother and Lord Krishna.

Notably, *Bhaben*, also addressed affectionately as '*Bhaben* Dada' by his peers, received great admiration from the zamindars (landlords) of Bengal. They would invite him to participate in significant dramas in Kolkata, where his violin-playing charmed the crowd, sometimes earning him a reward of fifty rupees. His artistic abilities were not limited to music; his drawings and various handicrafts also drew widespread admiration.

These details about *Bhaba Pagla* come from recounted stories by Manindra Mohan Saha, who observed *Bhaben*'s life up close, despite being two years his junior.

Bhaba Pagla, known for his rapid and skilled drawing, often left seasoned artists in awe. Manindra Mohan Saha recalled an instance when *Bhaba Pagla* was in the process of creating a statue of Maa Kali using bamboo pieces and clay. When his geography teacher suggested he might earn extra points if he crafted a globe instead, *Bhaba Pagla* wittily replied that the globe was meant for the very deity he was sculpting.

Word of *Bhaba Pagla's* talents and devotions spread throughout the village. Together with his brother Deben, they would sing devotional songs while wandering the village, gathering followers and soon becoming known as Gour and Nitai in Pakutia Village.

A noteworthy event occurred with the arrival of a new teacher, Shree Debendra Nath Hazra, from the Manikganj subdivision. Renowned for his devoutness and simplicity, Hazra supported a widow in his family and sought a spiritual experience. He dreamed of a divine message prompting him to go to Pakutia with the promise of a holy encounter.

Upon his anxious arrival in Pakutia, Hazra sought the whereabouts of the divine presence he was destined to meet. Local passersby, identifying his quest, directed him to B.C. High School, where he would find "Gour-Nitai." After meeting with Headmaster

Shree Kamakhya Basu and easily securing a teaching role due to his experience, Hazra was given accommodation adjacent to *Bhaba Pagla's* room.

The two would engage in religious discussions late into the night. On one memorable occasion at midnight, while everyone else slept, an emotional Hazra implored *Bhaba Pagla* to help him witness a vision of the goddess Kali. *Bhaba Pagla* instructed him to lie down like Lord Shiva, as Deben performed a ritual with flowers and leaves from the stone apple tree (Bel Pata)—both of which, along with other ritualistic items like a sword, were kept in *Bhaba Pagla's* room.

In the ritual, Hazra lay on the floor while *Bhaba Pagla* stood on his chest, sword in hand and chanting in a hushed voice. It was during this intense moment that *Bhaba Pagla* seemed to embody the Divine Mother, his tongue symbolically taking on her ferocious aspect as blood trickled down onto Hazra—a dramatic episode that solidified the mystical reputation *Bhaba Pagla* held in the community. Overwhelmed by the strange event Deben started to worship him with flowers and leaves of stone Apple tree. He offered flowers on the feet of *Bhabendra* according to his instruction.

After witnessing a divine vision of Goddess Kali, the bachelor Hazra Master remained unconscious for an entire night. The following morning, when word of the event spread, the school's teachers began to regard *Bhaben,* also known as *Bhaba Pagla,* with newfound respect.

From then on, Master Debendra Nath Hazra, in a show of reverence, would quietly enter *Bhaba Pagla's* room at night to anoint him with sandalwood paste and touch his feet. On occasion, when *Bhaba Pagla* awoke and protested, feeling unworthy as a student, Hazra Master would insist that although *Bhaba Pagla* was his student in the classroom, he was a spiritual master to him in all other aspects of life. Hazra Master found solace in spending a part of his salary to support *Bhaba Pagla* and Deben, after taking care of his own expenses and those of the widow in his care.

Bhaba Pagla would share various stories with Hazra Master, including one incident where, during the rainy season, he narrowly avoided stepping on a python, prompting his brother Deben to jest that he could have started a new episode reminiscent of Lord Krishna's dance on the serpent Kaliya. Another time, Deben suggested they both leave worldly matters behind and journey together to Brindaban, inspiring *Bhaba Pagla* to compose a song reflecting on the illusionary entanglements of life.

Manindra Mohan Saha further narrated how *Bhaba Pagla*, serving as the school's captain, maintained discipline during physical exercise drills. Teachers, out of deep respect, would salute *Bhaba Pagla*, causing him to feel embarrassed and insisting that he should be saluting them instead. Surprisingly, even outside the school premises, teachers persisted in saluting him, explaining that it was out of recognition for his spiritual stature.

It was common for *Bhaba Pagla* to have a playful habit of pinching his classmates, leading to the decision for him to sit on a separate bench. However, an upsetting incident occurred when a Muslim classmate placed a Fez cap on *Bhaba Pagla's* head as he arrived at school. Frustrated, *Bhaba Pagla* tried to remove it, but he was reprimanded by a teacher, Shree Suren Babu, who pulled his ear—a form of punishment *Bhaba Pagla* was not accustomed to. *Bhaba Pagla* expressed his objection to being treated thusly, and disheartened, he questioned the teacher's actions, hinting at the possibility of calling for his dismissal. Confused, the teacher inquired why *Bhaba Pagla* came to school wearing a cap typically associated with Muslims, not aware that it had been placed on his head by a classmate as a prank.

Upon having his ear pulled by Suren Sir, a teacher at the school, *Bhaba Pagla*, referred to affectionately as *Bhaben* Dada, was taken aback and reminded the teacher of the unwanted action in a calm manner. Despite this gentle reminder, he felt compelled to report the incident to the headmaster, questioning the appropriateness of Suren Sir's actions and hinting at potential repercussions for the teacher's career. Indeed, the following day Suren Sir resigned from his position. Before leaving, he presented *Bhaba Pagla* with various pencils as a parting gift.

If one delves deeper into the life story of *Bhaba Pagla*, we discover an existence that stands out as extraordinary and unparalleled among the incarnations of gods and revered personages in India. *Bhaba Pagla's* conduct, including the occasional use of the Bengali slang 'shaala', was unique to his character and set him apart. His school days at Pakutia came to an end, seemingly in anticipation of spiritual pursuits, similar to how Trambak Baba awaited the arrival of his disciple, Shyama Charan Lahiri, in the Himalayas.

Teachers, astounded by *Bhaba Pagla's* rapid and insightful responses to questions, would question their own ability to match his pace. *Bhaba Pagla* would explain that he did not depend on traditional learning but instead received a form of 'wireless communication' that presented him with living knowledge. He claimed that answers would materialize before him, and sometimes, he felt as if the Almighty Mother herself whispered the answers into his ear.

Bhaba Pagla's otherworldly wisdom and his extraordinary nature led people to wonder about his true identity. After being promoted to class VI, an unusual event occurred. At the designated bath time of 9 AM, *Bhaba Pagla* declared it was the moment for his 'bath of salvation.' In a swift, unexpected move, he ran away from the hostel. Despite efforts by the Hostel Superintendent, Shree Upendra Majumder, and the teachers, they were unable to follow him. *Bhaba Pagla* did not return to the school.

Thus, bringing his formal studies to a close, *Bhaba Pagla* embarked on a journey through the spiritual realm, venturing far beyond the confines of his domestic life.

****

CHAPTER 3

Udbodhan (The Name of Sarada Maa's House)

Bhaba Pagla's spiritual odyssey commenced with frequent visits to Kolkata, akin to the hidden spiritual flow of the Folgu River—an undercurrent that many often overlooked. His repeated visits to Kolkata facilitated his interactions with other divine personalities, establishing a spiritual lineage that featured revered figures, like Sarada Maa, the consort of the illustrious Sri Ramakrishna Paramahamsa.

During his early boyhood, *Bhaba Pagla*, also known by his given name *Bhaben*, and his brother Deben, became well-known figures in Shova Bazar, where they wandered, immersing themselves in spiritual songs of the Divine Mother and God, and engaging in kirtans devoted to Radha-Krishna. Their devotional fervor led neighbors to affectionately refer to them as 'Gaur' and 'Nitai', echoing divine names.

Sarada Maa resided at her house named 'Udbodhan', a sanctuary where people of all faiths—Hindus, Muslims, Christians, and Buddhists—gathered to hear her teachings. It was here that a connection between Sarada Maa and *Bhaba Pagla* blossomed.

A devout Krishna follower known as Tulsi, or Pagli Maa, often shared her spiritual exuberance through song and dance at Udbodhan. Upon discovering *Bhaba Pagla's* spiritual presence, she felt compelled to introduce him to Sarada Maa. When *Bhaba Pagla* consented to meet her, he entered the room exuding a divine aura, his delicate features and fair complexion likened to a young Nimai (another name for Chaitanya Dev). Spotting him, Sarada Maa exclaimed with delight at his angelic appearance and beckoned him closer.

Inquiring about his name, Sarada Maa listened intently as the boy introduced himself as *Bhaba Pagla,* elucidating the distinction between his being and his name with an enigmatic smile. When asked about the peculiar '*Pagla*' in his name, he wittily replied that it signified his unbounded spirit, playfully translating it as "free to move (Paa Alga)" in Bengali.

Throughout their conversation, *Bhaba Pagla* affirmed the fondness for his namesake, his laughter resonating in the room. Sarada Maa, intrigued by his joyful demeanour, encouraged him to sing. *Bhaba Pagla* acknowledged he had an abundance of songs, all original and divinely inspired, dismissing the need to perform the compositions of others such as Ramprasad. His songs, he revealed, were direct transmissions from the Divine Mother, which he simply transcribed and vocalized.

In crafting this seamless narrative, every pivotal moment is preserved, honouring the enchanting meeting between *Bhaba Pagla* and Sarada Maa, and capturing the essence of their spiritual discourse.

Bhaba Pagla, known in his youth as *Bhaben,* revealed to Sarada Maa the divine source of his songs, explaining that they were gifts from the Almighty Mother—what he saw he put down in writing, and what he heard, he transformed into song. Sarada Maa, thoughtful and visibly moved by the declaration that he had been receiving divine inspiration since the tender age of five, inquired further into his spiritual practices.

With a knowing smile, *Bhaben* responded to Sarada Maa's question regarding his devotion, whether it was to Goddess Kali or to Lord Krishna, by offering to sing a song encapsulating his understanding. The song he presented conveyed that Krishna and Kali are one and the same, transcending the duality and blindness of those who cannot fathom their unity. Through his poetic verses, he expressed the pointlessness of searching for good and bad of quarrelling without resolution, and suggested that those who cannot grasp the truth through intellect might do so through surrender and devotion.

Bhaben further illuminated this oneness with another song, which lovingly articulated the many names and forms of the divine—Shyam, Shyama, Shiba, Ram—each holding symbols like the bow, arrow, trishul, and flute. He sang of their various abodes, Ajodhya for Ram, Kashi for Shiba, Shree Brindavan for Shyam, and the crematorium for Mother Shyama. Through his verses, he depicted the rich tapestry of Hindu deities, each with unique attributes, yet connected by the underlying presence of the divine.

As he stayed at Bagbazar, *Bhaba Pagla* serenaded Sarada Maa with these profound song day after day, each one delving deep into the spiritual philosophy he embraced. Sarada Maa, captivated by the depth of his understanding and the beauty of his compositions, listened with amazement, recognizing the depth of spirituality that *Bhaba Pagla* possessed.

Sarada Maa often pondered over the identity and the profound philosophical insight of the boy, *Bhaben*, whose presence and songs instilled waves of joy in her heart, giving her a sense of divine bliss. *Bhaben* had a unique way of expressing his spiritual thoughts; he would open his arms wide in a welcoming gesture that no one had ever seen before, conveying his message in an embracing manner.

He was acutely attuned to the mood and atmosphere of those around him and could spontaneously compose songs that mirrored the sentiments of his audience. While in the presence of Sarada Maa, he crafted a song which implored the goddess to bestow kindness upon all, to gaze upon them fearlessly with her lotus-like eyes. He painted a vivid image of the goddess, whose presence was as intense as the colour of blood, and at whose feet lay the revered figure of Lord Shiva.

In his verses, *Bhaben* described the crematorium's flickering lights and the fervent devotion of those who dwell there, dissolving in worship amidst the pyres. Through his lyrics, he conveyed a sense of love that was as tender as it was powerful, a love that allowed both divine beings and demons to oscillate in the cradle of delight, with the entire cosmos and *Bhaba* himself swaying along in harmonious resonance.

Singing in the melody of Bhairabi Rag, he invoked the song he wrote at the age of six dedicated to Mother Kali. In this heartfelt plea, he expressed his inner turmoil and sought refuge and solace from the goddess. He sang of his reliance on her and her alone to soothe the ache in his heart as he approached the closing days of a chapter in his life.

These incidents and recitations from *Bhaben* to Sarada Maa capture his depth of devotion and the spiritual connection that enriched their every interaction. Each phrase and act of *Bhaben* underlined the transcendent bond between the earthly and the divine, making clear the magnitude of his inner spiritual journey.

Bhaben, with his tender voice, posed an introspective question in his song, imploring why Mother Kali remained distant from him. The song suggested a yearning for the divine presence to be closer. Upon hearing these soulful words, Sarada Maa offered high praise for the young saint.

He then presented his listeners with a riddle, asking who first referred to her as "Maa," which translates to "Mother." The audience was captivated by the question. *Bhaben* challenged them with the origin of such a loving term, suggesting that it was neither the grandfather nor any other familial relation that birthed the tender word "Mother." Rather, he proposed, it is a term that emerges spontaneously, with the power to transcend all pain and worldly divisions.

In his philosophical musings, *Bhaben* implied that the sacred syllable "Om" encapsulated the essence of maternal affection. By invoking the deity Munda Mali, another name for Goddess Kali, known for her garland of skulls, he depicted the goddess as the ultimate embodiment of love, which fills life to the brim with its purity.

Consistently integrating his spiritual life with his domestic existence, *Bhaba Pagla* wove his devotion into the fabric of his everyday life through his songs. He believed that the maternal bond is the nearest of all relationships—surpassing the closeness of siblings, spouses, teachers, or doctors—and expressed this through his composition:

"You are closest, Mother, You are closest, You revealed the world to me by your grace."

As he continued to sing spiritual hymns that resonated with his audience, curiosity arose about why he often included his name within his songs. It was an idiosyncrasy that underscored his personal journey with and through the divine—his songs were as much a signature of his identity as they were offerings to the divine.

When inquired about the peculiar habit of including his name in his songs, *Bhaben* explained to the curious onlookers with a semblance of simplicity that his name represented the number of his house. He drew a parallel to navigating the streets of Kolkata, where one must know a house's number to find it, indicating his name was a spiritual address of sorts. The spectators, marvelled at this young boy's profound spiritual insights and his ability in composition, discussed among themselves his source of learning and the identity of his guru.

Overhearing their musings, *Bhaben,* ever attentive to the discussions of the mundane world, declared that whoever invokes the name of Kali and can merge his mind into the divine, assumes the role of his spiritual teacher. He later composed a song, emphasizing that his true guru was the Almighty Mother, Bishwajana - a truth known to those who, understanding it, refrain from boasting about their enlightenment.

The young *Bhaben,* it seemed, was a spiritual tutor in his own right, imparting wisdom through stark simplicity, without recourse to scholarly texts. In a conversation, Sarada Maa reminisced about Paramhansa Dev, perhaps to gauge *Bhaben*'s views. His response that he did not hold an affinity for Paramhansa Dev, coupled with an anecdote where Paramhansa seemingly discarded money into water rather than offering it to the poor, prompted an outburst of laughter from Sarada Maa. It was *Bhaben*'s candidness and innocence that won over Sarada Maa's heart from day one.

Each day ended with a tender routine: Sarada Maa would cradle *Bhaben* in her lap, offering him treats like Mirchi (a type of crystallized sugar) and Chhana (a variety of cheese) by hand. This daily ritual, punctuated by the same question from Sarada Maa and the unchanging response from *Bhaben*—matched by his consistent bodily posture—brought about hearty laughter from Maa each time they interacted.

Before Sarada Maa could finish her inquiry, *Bhaben* interjected, "So let me see once," treating the matter as if it were routine. The following day, he arrived at Udbodhan and declared he had seen Thakur (Sri Ramakrishna), describing him standing with a cloth draped over one shoulder, depicted through an illustrative gesture.

Sarada Maa gazed at *Bhaben* with wonder and asked, "You saw him?" to which *Bhaben* confidently replied, "I have seen; He is very well." In the midst of their conversation, *Bhaben* mused, "The Mother (Almighty) has three eyes; I have two. So, it seems I wouldn't be able to see everything with the mere five." At that moment, Sarada Maa's gaze seemed to be searching for something profound.

A bystander noticed *Bhaben*'s restless demeanor and questioned if he was in search of something, maybe having lost an item. Prompted by the query, *Bhaben* broke into spontaneous song, embodying the yearning for the divine presence, resonating with those around him and arousing a profound sense of divine connection and wonder. People began to contemplate the deeper identity of this boy, whose compositions echoed those by luminaries like Ramprasad and Kamalakanta, known to summon the Mother Almighty in physical form through their devoted verses.

Sarada Maa was reminded of how Thakur Ramkrishna Dev cherished such songs, and how his disciple Naren and other associates often sang them, as they contained the essence of the Geeta, Upanishads, Vedas, and Vedanta. When asked about the source of his profound knowledge, *Bhaba Pagla* humbly responded, "He who resides within me, enlightens me."

Sri Ramakrishna, affectionately referred to as Thakur, was known for his worship of the idol of *Bhaba*tarini (Goddess Kali), carved from stone, which he reveres with such fervour as to bring it to life. Similarly, *Bhaben* used to sing these spirituals with natural simplicity and ease, embodying a wealth of knowledge that seemed beyond his years, as if ancient scriptures and philosophies had taken root in his young mind. It was as though the Mother not only enlivened the idol for Thakur but also awakened a profound spiritual consciousness within *Bhaben*.

Devotees who frequented Sarada Maa were drawn to the profound songs of *Bhaba Pagla*, which were dedicated to the Almighty Mother. One day, a devotee, inspired by the spiritual ambiance, questioned *Bhaba Pagla* on his approach to worshipping the Almighty Mother. *Bhaba Pagla's* countenance took on a serious expression as he contemplated the question.

In response, he sang a song that illustrated the depth of his devotion: to worship the Goddess with strength of mind and a heart full of unwavering devotion. He spoke of how the Goddess Avaya bestowed fearlessness and that the mysteries of Maa Kali's play were indeed profound. He shared that *Bhaba*ni, the embodiment of the goddess, whispered divine secrets to him, which he would then reveal openly to the supplicants.

Another restless devotee inquired about how to truly connect with Goddess Kali, how to call upon her. *Bhaba Pagla,* whose heart overflowed with love for Kali, offered another song. He described the experience of immersing oneself in the waters of devotion, sinking deep into the overwhelm of divine love, urging the mind to delve deep to find spiritual treasures. He assured that those who are submerged in divine love fear no storms or lightning; instead, they discover a realm of serenity and joy, transcending all earthly woes.

This prompted further curiosity among the devotees. One of them asked *Bhaba Pagla* if his devotion was exclusive to Kali, given his apparent indifference to other deities. *Bhaba Pagla* clarified, "I revere all forms of the divine, but I am particularly drawn to Kali." The same devotee then questioned why he would not feel the same for Goddesses Lakshmi, Saraswati, or Durga. *Bhaba Pagla* replied humorously that while all deities are without fault, his affinity for Kali was unique suggesting that her dark visage never betrayed any change, even in anger, unlike those with fairer complexions.

As time passed, the bond between *Bhaba Pagla,* Pagli Maa Tulsi, and the Udbodhan House continued to deepen, echoed by the sentiment 'Come Again'. However, a day arrived when *Bhaba Pagla* was unexpectedly absent. Known for being true to his word, his absence concerned everyone, including Sarada Maa. Upon his belated arrival, *Bhaba Pagla* explained he had been called away to

Dhaka and was now bound for Amta in East Bengal, guided by the will of the Almighty Mother.

Sarada Maa expressed her surprise at this sudden development. *Bhaba Pagla* playfully requested a parting gift, asking for a symbol with which he could pen his thoughts—a request that stirred an indescribable sentiment within Sarada Maa, understood only by her and the perceptive young saint.

Many were unaware of the profound internal thoughts of Sarada Maa, who, according to the teachings of Sri Ramakrishna, was in essence Bhagavati herself—the divine embodied as *Brahmamoyee.* Contrary to the beliefs held by some, Sarada Maa was not entirely devoid of literacy. An esteemed biographer noted that the daughter of *Bhaba* Mukherjee, a woman with elementary schooling, assisted Sarada Maa with her primary education. Within the seclusion of the women's quarters, two individuals would engage in reading and writing daily, and amongst them, Sarada Maa read texts like the Ramayana and the Mahabharata.

In the realm of saints and revered mothers, there is a heightened state of devotion; their engagement with language is rhythmic and intuitive. Traditional school education is not a prerequisite for them, as they possess the innate ability to grasp the musicality and rhythm of language through their willpower, mastering tones and melodies deemed impossible by others.

Bhaba Pagla was only five or six years old when he first presented his song of a 'Burning heart' to make Sarada Maa aware of his pain. One day, upon entering her room, he was gifted a slip of paper containing six engraved lines of verse by Sarada Maa—an expression of anguish that *Bhaba Pagla* treasured, placing it carefully within the temple.

When devotees inquired about its origin, *Bhaba Pagla* fondly recalled the kindness of Sarada Maa who had cradled him in her lap and fed him green grams and *Michhri*—a type of crystal sugar.

When questioned if the handwriting on the slip belonged to Sarada Maa, *Bhaba Pagla* explained that he wasn't sure, as the words were delivered to him by an elderly lady coming from within, who merely stated, "This is Maa's composition, to be given to you."

At that time, Jogin Mother and Gopal Mother were in the company of Sarada Maa. Interestingly, the slip bore no signature, only an inscription at the top declaring "Shree Maar Rachana" (Shree Maa's Composition). Later, when *Bhaben* asked Sarada Maa about this script, she responded in a soft voice that she didn't know much, simply acknowledging something was done. Over time, the writing faded, prompting the preservation of its essence through a photograph on 6th October 1972 (19th Aswin on the Friday of Mahalya, 1379 as per Bengali Calendar).

Labelled "Shree Maar Rachana" (Shree Maa's Composition), the piece conveyed a poignant plea to the mother to alleviate a debilitating pain:

"Oh Mother, take away this burden of pain. I am crumbling day by day under its weight, consumed by a tumultuous sorrow. My eyes overflow with tears, seeking solace from the coolness of water. With laboured breath, I persist, lighting the lamp with a fervent heart for the daily worship of Mother. In rhythmic dance, I offer my worship day and night. Now, I lay the garland of my agony upon your divine neck."

****

CHAPTER 4

Bhaba Pagla Returned to Amta and met His Childhood Companions

After spending around a year in Kolkata, *Bhaba Pagla* made his way back to Amta village, known to many as Amta, situated in the Dhaka district of East Bengal, now part of Bangladesh. Upon his return, a wave of excitement swept through those who had known him as a child. His childhood friends and companions, overcome with eagerness, hastened to greet him, their enthusiasm bordering on fervour.

Young and old alike flocked around *Bhaba Pagla*, drawn by the magnetism of his affectionate nature. The village felt enlivened as everyone from Bidhu, Nikunj, and Girija to Raman, Rebati, Hem, Kanu, Suresh, Satish, Sachindra, Phanindra, Sebendra, and Prafulla cherished the reunion with *Bhaben*, as they fondly called him, after a long separation.

Bidhu Chowdhury, Girija Roy, and other neighbourhood children shared innumerable memories of their days together—playing, walking, sleeping, and attending the primary school side by side.

The boy who was known for his innocent devotion, who offered clay-made *'Jilapi' or 'Jilebi'* and *'Sandesh'* sweets to the goddess Kali, was no other than their *Bhaben*. He would cover the plates of homemade sweets with a white cloth, and miraculously, at the end of his worship, the clay offerings would transform into real sweets of curdled milk cakes. The transformation was such that after the worship ended, everyone indulged in the delectable cakes that were once offerings.

Bhaba Pagla once candidly revealed the secret behind these miracles. He said, "I would call out to the 'Almighty Mother' with pure faith. She would touch the clay offerings, turning them real. To ensure that no one saw the divine hand of the Almighty Mother, I covered the plate with a white cloth."

Bhaben had a gift for music since he was five or six years old, composing songs to the divine Mother, stirring the souls of the young and old with his melodies. His musical talent extended beyond song to playing various instruments, including the harmonium, flute, and violin. The images of gods and goddesses sketched by *Bhaba Pagla* were extraordinary, as if the Goddess of learning herself guided his voice and hand. His gentle demeanour was beyond compare, captivating the hearts of all who knew him.

Bhaba Pagla, affectionately known as *Bhaben,* was surrounded by a sense of awe due to his miraculous birth. The faint smile and voice said to emanate from his mother's womb had already made him a figure of spiritual mystique in the eyes of his friends. As they grew, these friends were witnesses to *Bhaben*'s supernatural activities. Even at the tender age of seven or eight, *Bhaben*'s worship rituals in the crematorium and at school demonstrated his divine connection, leaving his companions to wonder at the depth of his unseen powers.

The sense of divinity around *Bhaben* only deepened when his friends reunited with him after a considerable time apart. Although his smile was as endearing as ever, a noticeable change had occurred: his songs to the Almighty Mother had grown more contemplative, more introspective, lifting him slightly out of their reach, while enhancing his allure day by day. This enigmatic transformation only increased their desire to have him join in their daily play.

During 'Nasta Chandra,' a Hindu festival celebrated on the full moon night in the month of Bhadra (corresponding to August or September), an event unfolded that etched itself into local lore. Sidhu and Girija, along with other companions, including *Bhaba Pagla*, planned to stealthily take pomelo fruits from the garden of Susila Sundari Devi, *Bhaben*'s senior aunt. Girija Sankar Roy, two years junior to *Bhaben*, sought to taste the fruits with a sense of pretend mischief.

Susila Sundari Devi's orchard was indeed a sight to behold, nestled in Pakur village with an abundance of trees and fruits. Her husband Keshab Mohan, senior to both Gajendra Mohan and Harendra Mohan, *Bhaben*'s father and uncle, respectively, resided in this lush garden. When *Bhaben* questioned the need to steal, Girija playfully insisted that the true fun lay in the thrill of the theft, infusing a sense of ceremony into their mischievous act.

As the night adventure unfolded, with the youngsters dashing ahead and *Bhaba Pagla* following, he encountered a figure posing as Girija. This apparition, who had earlier encouraged him to join in the theft, now implored him to abstain. *Bhaben*, confused by the sudden change, soon discovered that the genuine Girija had parted from him long before.

Bhaben was once again saved from potential harm, twice in quick succession, by a vigilant companion—first from a stack of wood that could have injured him and then from falling into a pit. On both occasions, Girija claimed to have seen the dangers clearly, although the reality of his presence was questionable.

When *Bhaben* finally reached the Chowdhury family home, he found Girija already there, sampling the pomelo fruits, which he had cut with a knife. The companion who had been at *Bhaben*'s side earlier had disappeared. It dawned on *Bhaben* that it was not Girija who had been with him, but the Almighty Mother in disguise.

This was just one among countless miraculous episodes surrounding *Bhaben*'s life. One such tale involved a schoolmate, Bidhubhushan Chowdhury. Struggling with arithmetic and facing the possibility of not advancing to the next grade, Bidhu sought *Bhaben*'s intervention with the headmaster, who had a soft spot for *Bhaben.* Initially hesitant, *Bhaben* ultimately consented to help after seeing the despair in Bidhu's eyes. As they approached the headmaster, Bidhu went ahead, leaving *Bhaben* behind, trusting in the influence *Bhaben* held.

Each incident, each interaction with *Bhaben,* seemed to intertwine the lives of his friends with threads of the extraordinary, further cementing *Bhaben*'s stature as a saintly figure in their midst.

Emboldened by *Bhaba Pagla's* assurances, Bidhubhushan set out for school, his spirit buoyed by the confidence he drew from *Bhaben*'s presence, even as he remained behind. Bidhubhushan approached the headmaster's room with trepidation but was greeted with an unexpected concern. "Oh, you have come. Come here, Bidhu," the headmaster beckoned, his next words surprising the boy, "I have not slept for three nights worrying about you."

Bidhubhushan was taken aback, especially when the headmaster revealed an astonishing turn of events: a mysterious '7' had appeared before a '0' in his arithmetic copybook, transforming his incorrect answers into correct ones—another miracle attributed to *Bhaben.* The headmaster preserved the arithmetic copy as a testament to this inexplicable phenomenon at the Pakutia school. Numerous other tales of *Bhaba Pagla's* devotees escaping harm—from robberies and tyrannical acts to confrontations with bandits and potentially fatal accidents—were attributed to their faith in his name.

In these stories, there was a consistent theme: *Bhaba Pagla* was a friend to all yet held no particular attachment. Bidhubhushan had observed this detached, enigmatic demeanour, which only added to the magnetic allure of *Bhaben*, from which it seemed impossible to disengage.

An unrelated episode further illustrated *Bhaben*'s miraculous interventions. One day, as Bidhubhushan and a friend walked along the bank of the Chowhati river, they encountered a crocodile exhibiting its wounded back above the water's surface. Bidhu recounted to *Bhaben* how Mani Babu, a local zamindar from Baliyati village, had attempted to hunt the crocodile and had injured it. The community buzzed with discussions about Mani Chowdhury's encounter with the crocodile, but Bidhu had a more compassionate take on the situation. He implored *Bhaben* to help heal the crocodile's wound.

Responding to the request, *Bhaben* instructed that a handful of mud be fetched from the riverbed. Forming the mud into a heap, *Bhaben* cast it onto the crocodile's wound while softly chanting "Kali, Kali." With a perfectly aimed toss, the healing mud hit its mark, and the crocodile disappeared beneath the waters.

Days later, the two friends were again strolling along the river when the very same crocodile approached, displaying its healed back to them—an apparent acknowledgment of *Bhaben*'s healing touch. Witnessing the closed wound, *Bhaben* saw that his work was successful and watched as the crocodile submerged itself once more, disappearing into the depths of the river.

Among his peers, *Bhaben*'s reputation for extraordinary acts grew, with stories of his name safeguarding followers from robberies, tyranny, and disasters. *Bhaba Pagla's* universal friendship was marked by an enigmatic detachment, yet his magnetic pull was irresistible. Even Surendra Ghosh of Nagpur, who thought *Bhaben* had lost his mind, contributed to his emerging identity as *Bhaba Pagla*, a moniker that suggested divine madness—a name that even Maa Kali herself seemed to whisper as an endearment.

Withdrawing from worldly education, *Bhaba Pagla* secluded himself in a secret room of his family home—an area where valuables were stored and thus named. There, he dedicated his days and nights to worship, meditation, and composing songs in honour of the Almighty Mother. His practice was not the repetition of mantras or scriptures, but the outpouring of heartfelt melodies.

One day, during an intensely spiritual moment, *Bhaba Pagla* was stunned to witness a large python in the room. Yet, unlike others who may have succumbed to fear, he maintained a unique calmness, addressing the creature with an unflinching stare. Murmuring 'Kali' thrice in a distinct tone, he watched as the python transformed into the beautiful, benign figure of Goddess Kali, who appeared before him with a reassuring gesture, only to vanish after his heartfelt plea for her continued presence when called upon.

While *Bhaben* was immersed in the spiritual world, his sudden departure from school sparked controversy among his relatives and neighbours. His elder brother Girindra Mohon expressed annoyance, and the whispers reached *Bhaben*'s ears. Distressed by the judgements and dishonour from those around him, he expressed his despair and yearning for the goddess's acceptance through poignant songs, pleading for her embrace and reprieve from the burn of worldly scorn. In his music, the depth of *Bhaba Pagla's* inner turmoil was as tangible as tears, a reflection of a soul caught between earthly trials and heavenly communion.

Amidst a life fraught with sin and sorrow, *Bhaba Pagla,* known as *Bhaben,* expressed his lament through a soul-stirring song, reaching out to Mother Tara. His lyrics, "How long shall I stay to bear the burden of sin; Oh, Mother Tara, life ends with sorrow after sorrow. No more can I tolerate the sorrow," resonated with profound pain and rhythmic anxiety that moved everyone who heard it, particularly causing distress to his mother, Gayasundari

Devi. She had taken note of her son's growing disinterest and disdain for worldly matters.

One day, Gayasundari Devi overheard a conversation between *Bhaben* and his friends. A friend questioned, "Did you take birth again in the district of Dhaka?" *Bhaba Pagla* confirmed, "Yes, my friend, not far from Amta, in the family of weavers in Bhatara village." When asked if he remembered those words, *Bhaba Pagla* affirmed, "I remembered. The Mother Almighty made me remember."

Intrigued, Gayasundari Devi approached *Bhaben* for clarification. *Bhaben* responded, "If you don't believe, go to the house of Haricharan Basak at Bhatara and ask if their son named Amar Chand died a few years ago." He assured her that, despite not being as wealthy, the Basak family had a double-storied cemented house.

This revelation quickly spread beyond their immediate circle, reaching the Basak household. The parents of Amar Chand visited the Chowdhury family at Amta to meet *Bhabendra* Mohon, who corroborated his previous life, describing a specific kite reel with red and blue string still in their possession. His accuracy caused a stir in the community as the reel was indeed found in the Basak's home.

This disclosure unsettled Gayasundari Devi, who feared losing *Bhaben* as she had lost Amar Chand. Considering *Bhaben* the jewel of her life, she panicked and sought an astrologer's counsel, anxious her son might meet an untimely fate.

Bhabendra Mohon, grappling with the concept of his reincarnation, grew intensely aware of the debates surrounding him. He was perplexed by the complexity of worldly life and pained that his purpose in being reborn wasn't understood, evoking a sense of alienation even among his loved ones. This misunderstanding fuelled his urge to leave his body once more.

Bhaba Pagla's actions reflected a sense of urgency: he composed songs swiftly, expected answers without delay, and his thoughts quickly turned to action, demonstrating an inability to endure waiting.

One night, as everyone slept, *Bhaba Pagla* walked the floor alone, knife in hand, mumbling, "Why did I come here? What have I done here?" In this moment of solitude, he crafted a poignant song, "Fly away, baby bird, now in the blue sky. Oh, does anyone love you, sitting in the cage?" There, in the quiet of night, *Bhaba Pagla's* identity as a nurtured soul seeking freedom was captured in his mournful melody.

In the depth of the night, a troubled *Bhaba Pagla,* known as *Bhaben,* found himself wrestling with his purpose, murmuring, "Why did I come here? What have I done here?" These questions gave rise to a melancholic song, where he contemplated the plight of a caged bird yearning for the freedom of the blue sky.

At one o'clock at night, with a restless mind and heavy heart, *Bhaben* ventured outside, clutching a long knife. He made his way to the sacred Gab tree, a site where he had performed worship and witnessed the transformation of mud 'Sandesh' cakes into sweet, curdled milk cakes through the touch of the Almighty Mother—a place wrapped in cherished memories.

Standing under the Gab tree for a moment, he looked up to see a rope hanging from one of its branches. Acting on impulse, he quickly ascended the tree, tested the rope's strength by pulling it several times, and, after making sure it was secure, tied a knot and placed it around his neck. With the chant of "Kali, Kali, Kali," he attempted to end his life.

As the dawn broke, the night gave way to the morning light, and *Bhabendra* was found lying beneath the holy Gab tree. The gentle morning breeze caressed him as though it were a maternal touch, and he lay there as if in a deep slumber.

When the news of the event reached the household, Gayasundari Devi rushed out to her son, forsaking all else. She found *Bhaben* and scooped him into her arms. He awoke, giving a vacant glance that led the onlookers to suspect he had lost his memory.

Surprised to find her son on the ground rather than hanged, both mother and son noticed the torn rope dangling from the tree. *Bhaben,* with no recollection of the ordeal, wondered where the part of the rope that he had knotted around his neck was. Upon lifting his gaze, he spotted a garland of fresh 'Beli' flowers lying where his head had been.

Overcome with emotion, tears streamed down his cheeks as he realized the harsh rope had transformed into a garland of 'Beli' flowers. He tenderly took the garland, touched it to his head, and then placed it on his chest.

His mother, filled with urgency, pressed him for answers: "What is this, my son? What happened? Who gave you this garland? What did you do?" In his characteristic transparency, *Bhaba Pagla,* a man who kept no secrets and hid nothing, showed the torn rope to her and confessed without any shame, "I hung that rope around my neck, and after hanging myself, I lost consciousness."

The incident left a trace of the miraculous, an impression of divine intervention that had averted what could have been a tragic end for *Bhaba Pagla.*

****

CHAPTER 5

Oh, Mother (Almighty Goddess), You want to shackle a Dear of the Forest?

In Kolkata, Gajendra Mohan, *Bhaba Pagla's* father, had many distant family members. One wealthy widow, a landlady residing at 13 Nath Bagan Street, whose landlord husband had passed away, was related to *Bhaba Pagla*. Her husband used to own land in the Baliyati village of the Dhaka district. Remaining in Kolkata after his death, she was well-off, with an idol of God housed within her residence. Hearing that *Bhaben* had left school and showed no interest in pursuing monetary gains, yet finding there was a slight need for money in their household, the aunt thought of *Bhaben*. She was aware of *Bhaben*'s inclination towards serving godly idols and felt it would be apt for him to take over the worship responsibilities in her home. Additionally, she recognized the advantage of having a young man at home for emergency errands.

The aunt extended an invitation to *Bhaben* through a letter: "Will you come to stay at my home in Kolkata? You can perform the worship of the Almighty Mother here. You will be provided with food and lodging, and in addition, I will give you twenty rupees per month for your personal expenses. As I am a lady alone, you can also assist with the marketing, while spending your time in prayer at home." *Bhaben* agreed to her proposal after getting consent from his mother, Gayasundari Devi, and soon presented himself at her doorstep at house number 13 in Nath Bagan. He took up the duty of serving the idol of God.

Bhaben began to enchant the household with chants and songs dedicated to the Almighty Mother that he had composed himself. News of his presence in Nath Bagan spread to the nearby Sova Bazar area, attracting crowds to the house to hear him. His aunt occasionally interrupted his prayerful singing in the evenings with requests for her to run errands.

After one month, a small incident took place. The rich aunt handed *Bhaben* only eight rupees instead of the promised twenty. Internally, *Bhaba Pagla* smiled at this act, and inspired by the situation, he composed a song: "Oh Mother (Almighty), you wish to bind a wild deer with but eight hands of thread, yet freedom always abides in the forest. The deer thrives on green grass, its body growing robust grazing upon it. None can capture it."

This reflected *Bhaben*'s spirit and philosophy that true freedom was not confined by material constraints, a testament to his spiritual outlook on life.

In the song he created, *Bhaba Pagla* spoke of the freedom of the forest. He compared the inhabitants of the forest, metaphorically represented by a black woman, to the wild deer. They cherished the shadows and the calm that the forest provided, far from the decay of man-made structures. They luxuriated in the cool breeze of the lush greenery, under the protective gaze of Mother Shyama, the Almighty Mother. *Bhaba Pagla* expressed through his song that he was meant to praise her always, suggesting that the confines of city life were not for him.

The song, written, composed, and performed by *Bhaba Pagla,* reflected his genuine approach to life; he harboured no fear, no shame, and concealed nothing. His music was an act of worship, and the grace of 'Mother' served as a conduit for imparting lessons.

Despite his devotion, the landlady imposed mundane tasks upon him, such as cleaning the latrine, which *Bhaben* undertook without complaint. As her demands grew, she asked *Bhaben* to collect cow dung from the streets after a morning walk. The night passed, and the next morning, as he contemplated the task and sought guidance from *Brahmamoyee*, the Almighty Mother, a heap of cow dung was mysteriously found at the doorstep of the house at dawn.

When the main door opened, the sight perplexed everyone, leaving the landlady and her household in wonder as to who could have gathered and deposited such a pile at such an hour. Unlike the others, *Bhaba Pagla* was neither surprised nor disturbed. Tears came to his eyes as he recognized the divine intervention on his behalf, believing that the mother herself had gathered the cow dung for him.

Moved by this act of solidarity and support from the divine, *Bhaba Pagla* internally voiced, "In the end, I made you collect cow dung, Mother (Almighty). Oh Mother, you gathered it from one street to another for me. No, I cannot stay at this house, not even for a moment." With that, he decided to leave the land-lady's house, departing from there permanently.

From Nath Bagan to Sova Bazar Street:

A short distant away, nestled within the same vicinity stood an illustrious building at 4 Shova Bazar Street, owned by esteemed Roy-Chowdhury, Zamindar family.

In North Kolkata, *Bhaba Pagla's* elder brother, known as Girindra Mohan, had made a name for himself by expertly performing 'Kirtan'—a devotional song praising Lord Krishna. He was a skilled player of the 'Mridangam' and country-made drums, and his devotion was apparent both in his physical form and in his behaviour, truly embodying the principles of a 'Vaishnav' (a disciple of Lord Krishna).

Bhabendra Mohan, often referred to as *Bhaben,* would happily accompany his elder brother to various functions to assist or co-perform, greatly enhancing the events with their combined presence. His role often entailed supporting Girindra Mohan in different religious and cultural gatherings.

Among the residents of Shyambazar in Kolkata was a distinguished lady known for her devotion to Lord Krishna. Nicknamed 'Lady Gouranga' because of her fair complexion, she had once been part of a wealthy family before becoming a widow. She dedicated herself to religious activities and had been absorbed in the stage of meditation for many years.

Lady Gouranga's residence was located off Cornwallis Street, which was later renamed as 'Bidhan Sarani'. Known for organizing functions celebrating the divine, she often invited the respected saint Girindra Mohan to perform Kirtan at these gatherings to chant the name of Lord Krishna.

Bhabendra Mohan, as well, was frequently requested to accompany his elder brother at such functions, especially when Girindra Mohan had commitments to other events. The significant contributions made by *Debendra* and *his* younger brother, were indeed unparalleled.

One memorable occasion was the 'Dol Purnima' celebration—a festival coinciding with the full moon, where Girindra Mohan was a distinguished performer. *Bhabendra* also attended that day, contributing to the spiritual ambiance. During this celebration, a picture, which had been venerated by the devotees for many days, was displayed, adding to the occasion's reverence. The Kirtan went on for an extended period, reflecting the depth of devotion and the significance of the ceremony.

At times, *Bhabendra* Mohan would be requested to accompany his elder brother to these events, especially when Girindra had other engagements. The younger brother's extraordinary involvement in these sacred festivities could not be overstated.

A particularly notable event was the 'Dol Purnima' festival, aligning with the full moon, where Girindra Mohan was a prominent participant. *Bhabendra* was present that day as well, contributing to the sacred atmosphere. Highlighting the event was a revered picture that had been the focus of devotional attention for many days. As the Kirtan continued well into the gathering, it epitomized the profound spirituality and solemnity of the celebration.

Known for her fair complexion, the widow in Shyambazar came to be addressed as 'Lady Gouranga.' Her home was situated on what was then Cornwallis Street, which would later be renamed Bidhan Sarani. She was a patron of religious gatherings, often hosting and overseeing Kirtan ceremonies devoted to the chant of Lord Krishna's name.

Girindra Mohan, a saint, was frequently invited by Lady Gouranga to lead the Kirtan functions in her house. Due to his multiple commitments, Girindra Mohan occasionally requested that his younger brother, *Bhabendra* Mohan, accompany him to these functions.

The contributions of *Bhabendra Mohan*, who was recognized for both his musical skill in Kirtan and his spiritual presence, were unparalleled. Girindra Mohan, another famous Kirtan musician and *Bhaben*dra's elder brother, attended a significant function at a temple during 'Dol Purnima,' a festival marked by the full moon. *Bhabendra* was also present on that day and had long been venerated by the devotees.

During this vibrant occasion, devotees engaged with zealous devotion, throwing 'Aabir'—a colourful powder—on the idol, inadvertently covering the deity's picture in a dense layer of powder, obscuring its eyes, nose, and face. *Bhaba Pagla,* witnessing their fervour, was quick to recognize the unintended oversight.

He cautioned the crowd, exclaiming in concern that they were covering Gouranga's face with the powder. To remedy the situation, *Bhabendra* leaned forward and gently blew the Aabir from the picture's face. The head priest reacted with alarm, shouting out, "Ah! You've blown air from your mouth onto the picture of God. Have you not spittled upon it?"

*Bhaben*dra, acknowledging the priest's concern with a hint of irony, replied, "Oh, is it so? Have I spittled?" He then urged his elder brother to stop the songs, calling for an immediate halt to the music. Raising his right hand, he covered the mouth of the singing saint, gesturing with surprise, he said, "By opening the mouth to sing songs, won't spittle fall on the idol then?"

Through this interaction, *Bhabendra* conveyed the idea that the essence of worship lies beyond strict formalities, and that devotion should be considerate and mindful.

Bhaba Pagla enjoyed engaging the devotees with wit and humour. He would often draw an analogy, saying, "Just as you consume tak (something sour, like 'a curd-based drink) to aid digestion after a meal, similarly, I talk (referring to the Bengali word 'tak' for sour) to impart spiritual knowledge through my songs." However, his humour sometimes made the kirtan player, Girindra Mohan—referred to here as the 'Girin saint'—anxious. Not everyone was familiar with *Bhaba Pagla's* younger brother, *Bhaben,* whose whims could potentially disrupt the Kirtan if he chose so, as it was believed the gods and goddesses adhered to his desires and aversions.

Bhaben pondered over how those entangled in false beliefs and misconduct could recognize the wonders performed by *Bhaba Pagla.* Yet many had come to realize his significance and thus he was frequently invited to temples and homes, where people eagerly awaited his songs and discussions. Conversations with *Bhaben* often led to diverse questions and enlightening answers.

On one occasion, *Bhaba Pagla* was honoured with an invitation to a house in Shyambazar. Wherever he went, there was an atmosphere of melody and genial conversation. The room dedicated to worship at this particular house was small, with images of gods affixed to earthen pots and framed depictions adorning the walls. Rekha, a devotee, was responsible for the maintenance of this sacred space. *Bhaba Pagla,* given the title '*Pagla*' affectionately by devotees, found himself enveloped within this room. His presence elicited joy and good spirits, making the attendees laugh with his playful words, as when he jested that they should not spit in the temple and interrupt the kirtan.

During the gathering, a devotee inquired of *Bhaba Pagla,* "Which god is the most beautiful?" To which *Bhaben* replied, "Which god is not beautiful? Please give me a moment; I am composing a song." *Bhaba Pagla* quickly crafted a new song and accompanied it with the harmonium, treating the tune as a chanting mantra to welcome the Almighty Mother.

Bhaba Pagla instructed the people to be quiet during his harmonium performance and singing, warning that any disturbance could metaphorically 'break the leg' of the dancing Mother. On the day in question, he began to sing a newly composed song with a harmonious tune: "The handsome Krishna, the godly Kali, the beautiful Shiva, the pleasing Rama."

His cautionary remarks were not just about maintaining silence; they were to prevent disruption of the divine harmony. When the music resonated properly, it was as if it lured the Almighty into a dance, and any gossip or idle talk could disrupt this sacred act, an act so exquisite it was said to be miraculous, and worthy of later discussion.

****

CHAPTER 6

The Temple of 'Kali' (Goddess) at Amta

Bhaba Pagla traveled between Amta and Kolkata as he pleased, with his divine play unfolding in both locations. Often, his activities and intentions escaped the understanding of the laypeople. To ensure he wouldn't vanish, his mother, Gayasundari Devi, accompanied him, though she also needed to oversee the property, manage associated personnel, and attend to the servants at their estate in the village of Amta, within the Dhaka district of Bangladesh.

During this time in Amta, *Bhabendra* Mohan, also known as *Bhaben,* initiated a new venture, forming a musical group with his schoolmates. Girija Sankar Roy, an associate of *Bhaben,* provided colourful insights into their assembly. The student musicians, averaging 16 to 17 years of age, saw *Bhaba Pagla* on the violin, Girija on the harmonium, Madhu and Bhasani on the bamboo flute, Digamali Baithya on the tabla and dholak, Girindra Karmakar on the khol, and Ramesh Sarkar on the santoor and kartal. The group, comprised of both Hindu and Muslim students, participated in *Bhaba Pagla's* concerts with divine joy.

Bhaba Pagla wrote songs that embraced the essence of Bhagavan, Allah, and God, emphasizing that there was no distinction between Allah and Ishwar. The concerts gained fame, particularly for *Bhaba Pagla's* skillful violin playing. Eventually, *Bhaben* expressed a wish to construct a temple dedicated to the goddess Kali. This proposition reached Girindra Mohan, the eldest brother and de facto head of the family after their father's passing.

Family members initially hesitated at the idea of building another temple, given the existing 'Chandi Mandap' for Goddess worship and a place for Durga and other festivals. However, they also recognized that opposing *Bhaba Pagla's* wishes, would not bode well, as he made no distinction between family and others in any matter.

A crisis arose when the youngest of Girindra Mohan's sons, just one and a half years old, fell severely ill with measles. With the disease worsening and hopes dimming, the family despaired. At this critical juncture, Girindra Mohan approached *Bhaben*, offering to build the temple if his brother could save the sick child. *Bhaben* remained silent, yet, over time, the child miraculously recovered, much to the family's relief.

Radhakund Devi, Girindra Mohan's wife, looked upon her brother-in-law with immense gratitude. She questioned whether her baby would survive, informed by the pain of previously losing two children prematurely. To this, *Bhaben* assured, "Well, I am selecting your son's name. You need not fear." His words provided comfort to Radhakund, still reeling with anxious tears.

Bhaba Pagla went on to name the nephews in sequence—Gour Mohan, Gobinda Mohan, Gadadhar, Gokul Mohan, Golok Mohan, and Gopi Mohan—prefacing each name with the initial "G" to honour their grandfather Gajendra Mohan and father Girindra Mohan.

Eventually, Girindra Mohan began the construction of the temple but disregarded *Bhaba Pagla's* location preference, aiming to minimize expenses. Despite this divergence from the original plan, the temple building commenced.

However, the temple that Girindra Mohan had begun to build ultimately collapsed. Recognizing his error in not following his younger brother *Bhaben*'s advice, Girindra entrusted the reconstruction to *Bhaben.* Pleased, *Bhaba Pagla* eagerly engaged in the temple's erection. He selected the location for the new temple to be just south of the sacred 'adi' tree, outside the house. *Bhaba Pagla* designed a small temple, measuring 10 feet square with a height of 4 feet.

The temple had an entrance facing south, adjacent to a path used by the villagers. The low height of the entrance required the devotees to bow as they entered, a symbolic gesture of reverence before observing the statue of the Goddess Kali within. *Bhaba Pagla* devoted himself to the temple's decoration, the establishment of the clay statue of Kali, and the worship of the Almighty Mother 'Kali'. Consequently, his interactions with the household diminished as he spent much of his time in the temple.

Adjacent to the temple, he constructed a 9 by 8-foot room facing west, near a garden brimming with flowers. Here, *Bhaba Pagla* would rest, compose songs, sing, and speak with visitors. Even Gayasundari Devi, his mother, would approach the temple to inquire about his daily meal preferences. Standing at the door, she would watch her son immersed in composing music and, during leisure, ask, "What type of food would you like today?"

For many days, *Bhaben* responded not with words but with signs. The ringing of a bell signified his desire for 'Ghanto,' a mixed vegetable and rice dish. The sound of a conch implied he wanted 'Shaak,' a leafy vegetable dish. The utterance of 'Tak, Tak' indicated his craving for sour curry. A pat on his body signaled a request for a solid vegetable mixture known as 'Charchari.' In this manner, he conveyed his culinary choices of over one hundred and eight different food items. On a particular day, he signaled he would be satisfied with just one specific dish. After discerning her son's wish, Gayasundari would return inside to prepare it, allowing *Bhaba Pagla* to resume his work.

To the south of the Kali temple stood a worship space, known as the Naat temple, and to its east was another flower garden. The theatrical troupe that *Bhaba Pagla* and his childhood friends had formed continued to evolve, culminating in the production of 'Krishna Leela,' dramatic portrayals of Lord Krishna's life. The troupe's first theatrical play was 'Britrasur Badh,' followed by 'Bijoy Basanta,' amongst others.

Girija Shankar Roy, a classmate of *Bhaba Pagla*, recounted their performances of various dramas such as 'Sita,' 'Harish Chandra,' 'Kedar Roy,' 'Pather Sheshe,' 'Baman Avataar,' and 'Ananta Mahatma.' Remarkably, *Bhaba Pagla* once performed the role of a woman in 'Ananta Mahatma.' Inspired by these experiences, *Bhaba Pagla* composed a song celebrating those who remind him of life's final act, acknowledging their wisdom and friendship.

The villagers were entranced by the theatrical performances. *Bhaba Pagla*, in his devotion, worshipped tirelessly, summoning the presence of the Almighty Mother. Legend has it that the Goddess herself, moved by such heartfelt invocation, had once mended the fence of the poet Ramprasad. Such is the power of devoted summons from the heart.

The revered Kenduli of Birbhum District in West Bengal situated on the bank of the Ajoy River offers a backdrop for the story of Joydev, who became known as a saint through the grace of Lord Krishna. As the month of 'Aashar' approached, marking mid-June to mid-July, preparations for the annual Rath Jatra, a significant Hindu festival celebrating Lord Jagannath, began in Dhamrai, Bangladesh. Lord Jagannath, considered an incarnation of Lord Vishnu and one part of the holy Hindu Trinity, is honoured in a celebration only paralleled by the Puri Rath Jatra.

Each year, a grand fair accompanies the festival at Dhamrai. *Bhaba Pagla* was persuaded by friends to attend, a sentiment not shared by his elder brother Girindra Mohan, a saint in his own right, who felt that seeing his brother *Bhaben* was akin to seeing the holy chariot itself and thus did not feel compelled to visit the fair. Despite their urgings, citing his devotion and skill in kirtan, Girindra expressed that he saw the divine in *Bhaben*'s ability to make the goddess Kali dance, musing that while he himself was engaged in calling upon Krishna, *Bhaben* was immersed in devotion to Kali.

As the group planned their trip to Dhamrai, *Bhaba Pagla* was not particularly enthusiastic but agreed to go, acquiescing to the wishes of his devotees. Alone at the fair on the following morning, *Bhaba Pagla* was struck by a divine vision admonishing him for leaving the temple in Amta without proper guardianship. He swiftly returned to find that the nun he had trusted with the worship had inadvertently damaged the eyes of the earthen idol of the Mother. With heartfelt sorrow and sealed doors, he repaired the idol, restoring its eyes with paint.

Following this incident, *Bhaba Pagla* expressed a desire to establish an idol made of black stone. Ganga Charan Saha offered financial support for its creation, seeking and gaining *Bhaba Pagla's* approval. Despite an earnest search in Dhaka and failing to find the black stone, Ganga Charan was directed by *Bhaba Pagla* to meet with Bhaskar in Kolkata, a prominent merchant in Kalighat Bazaar. Initially unsuccessful, Ganga Charan was later instructed by *Bhaba Pagla* to dig in a specific place behind the merchant's shop, resulting in the miraculous discovery of the desired black stone.

The idol was crafted with care and devotion by sculptors and completed in due time. Ganga Charan brought the finished statue to Amta amidst a procession of followers. *Bhaba Pagla* joyously welcomed the idol named 'Anandamoyee' (Mother of Happiness) to the temple, with the ceremony accompanied by the rhythmic beats of drums and the chiming of bells. The magnificent black stone idol, situated on a semi-spherical platform, faced south, inviting all to view and venerate it. *Bhaba Pagla* envisaged that white bangles of conch shells would adorn her wrists beautifully, contrasting with her dark form.

As *Bhaba Pagla* instructed, the conch shopkeeper in Dhaka was ordered to craft exquisite bangles with a locking mechanism specially designed for the Mother's wrists. When the conch bangles arrived, *Pagla* immediately adorned the Mother with them, marveling at how beautiful they looked. However, the bangles unexpectedly opened and fell from the Mother's wrists. No matter how many times he attempted to secure them, the same thing happened. *Bhaba Pagla* later shared this incident, recounting the words of the Almighty Mother. She explained to him that as her children are scattered across the globe, she embraces them all; they are her branches ("shakha" in Bengali) and sub-branches ("prashakha"). Hence, she proclaimed no need for the conch bangles ("shakha").

One day, a remarkable event occurred. A seller peddling conch bangles came to *Bhaba Pagla's* house, offering bangles for the Mother in the temple. While *Pagla* scrutinized the bangles, he discovered a small polishing tool to improve their gloss. At that moment, he had a vision and identified the vendor as none other than Lord Shiva in disguise. *Pagla* chose to keep the bangles despite the incident.

The seller requested payment, to which *Bhaba Pagla* agreed — on the condition that the seller would join him for lunch at noon. The conch seller, with a knowing smile, agreed but mentioned he would return later. As noon passed and the seller did not reappear, *Bhaba Pagla* chuckled to himself acknowledging that even Lord Shiva, in his attempt to be coy, could not fool him, and considered this realization an act of divine grace.

True to his word, as God is always truthful, the conch seller did return as promised, leaving *Bhaba Pagla* assured of Mahadev's (God's) grace and blessings.

During this period, *Bhaba Pagla* was often invited to nearby villages such as Baliaati, Baliya, and Ketharpur to spread the divine messages through song and to encourage the villagers towards good conscience and salvation. On one occasion, as he journeyed to Ketharpur, he visited the home of Rohini Sadhu, which was a hub for many devotees.

Pagla was traveling through a vast meadow that stretched three miles from Nayachar to Thimukha, in the region of Pakutia village. A young man in his prime, *Pagla* traversed the field swiftly, moving at an impressive speed of ten miles per hour. Adorned with worship garlands hanging from his neck, he carried a majestic golden bamboo stick covered in gold and studded with precious jewels and pearls, which measured five feet in length. His long hair, gathered into a bunch, swayed against his back with each step he took, while the garlands on his neck brushed against his chest in rhythm with his gold-covered stick. As the midday sun blazed overhead, he perspired profusely.

Despite the deserted meadow, a voice suddenly called out, "Hey." Startled, *Bhaba Pagla* stopped — it was uncommonly disrespectful to address him in such a manner. He wondered who would dare to be so ill-mannered in this area and whether there was anyone who did not recognize him as *Bhaba Pagla.*

As *Bhaba Pagla* gazed upward, he noticed a striking man standing nearby. This man exuded a divine presence yet initiated a casual conversation. *Pagla* shared an experience he had while walking blindfolded across the field from Nayachar to Thimukha. His pace was so swift that the bunch of long hair and the garlands on his neck flapped against his back and chest, respectively. Traveling at a remarkable speed of ten miles per hour, he was surprised when a voice cut through the silence, asking, "Hey, who goes there braving the scorching sun?"

In response, *Pagla* addressed the stranger as 'brother' and shared his perspective: "I am a man of the Jungle, akin to an animal in the forest. How is it that you understand me, brother? Indeed, she is a wild daughter, the queen of the forest, yet she aids me. Amidst the sweltering heat of the noon sun, as I move from one meadow to another, she appears over me. That small sun, the Almighty Mother, she becomes the great sun of a million suns sheltering me. To me, she is like a Almighty mother and in the evening, I contemplate her."

Bhabha *Pagla*, though a man of the jungle, had not lost his senses. Even the true cobra would hiss at the sight of his conch garlands and golden stick, respecting the rhythmic and principled words he lived by.

His amazement grew when he noticed that the handsome man possessed a beautiful snake draped around his neck and wielded a trident. Before *Pagla* could reflect further, he was greeted with affectionate words from the stranger, asking if the one who resides within his soul suffered from the intense heat.

Struck by the kindness in the man's voice, Bhabha *Pagla* listened intently. The voice instructed him to accept a holy mantra for initiation. The kind stranger delivered into *Pagla's* ears the sacred initiation words of 'Brahma' (the god of creation) and the powerful name of goddess Kali for salvation.

The account of *Bhaba Pagla's* initiation by Lord Shiva was recorded on Sunday, 17th July 1983, at the *Bhaba*ni temple in Kalna. Present were disciples and followers including Gopal Chandra Bandopadhyay, an affiliate of Calcutta University; Sathay Chand Chowdhury, a devoted councillor to Pagla; and Shrimati Joli Ghatak, who had served for fifteen years; along with other distinguished persons and adepts.

From songs composed by *Bhaba Pagla*, we discern the identity of his Guru. He expresses that even though one might speak of gods, the Guru is supreme. He declares that Deva Maheshwar is the Guru of Shri Ram Chandra, articulating that it is not easy to equal the Guru, who in this instance, is Shiva, revered as Mahadeva.

Pagla also crafted another song asserting his guru's universality; a secret known only to those beyond words. In this verse, *Pagla* entreats the guru for mercy, as he persists in his devotion.

Over time, *Bhaba Pagla* established an Annual Festival in honour of the Almighty Mother, referred to as 'Anandamoyee'. The celebration was scheduled to take place on the last Saturday of Baishakh (the Bengali month spanning Mid April to Mid May).

Bhaba Pagla would enthusiastically announce, "The worship of the Mother will be held on the last Saturday of Baisakh (Mid April to Mid May). Please do come." Every year, people from all walks of life would flock to the annual function without discrimination – Christians, Hindus (Brahmin, Kshatriya, Shudra, Vaishya alike), alongside scholars, illiterates, the rich, and the poor. All were welcome to partake in the 'mahaprasada' (the sacred holy meal) of Anandamoyee, the Almighty Mother. The festivities transformed into a grand fair, drawing in thousands to gather in a delightful assembly, accompanied by a musical ensemble of one hundred and eight hand drum players.

The distribution of the holy meal was truly a spectacle. Devotees contributed groceries and vegetables, and it remained a mystery how such abundant supplies were collected and by whom. With joyous hearts, many disciples and believers served throughout the festival. After the day of worship, the celebration would continue for an entire month with theatrical plays in the open fields, music, songs, and a vibrant fair. The temple of 'Kali' (the Goddess) stood as a hub of religious and cultural activities, eagerly anticipated by the local villagers for the following year's festival.

It must be noted that *Bhaba Pagla's* customs did not align with traditional practices of engaging Brahmin priests or animal sacrifice. Each year, the festivities began with a procession to fill the 'welfare pitcher' with water from the bank of the river Chowhati. This procession, featuring hand-drum players and a worship flag, captivated and drew in thousands of joyful participants. The exact moment when *Pagla* would start the procession was never declared, though his closest disciples noticed that he would become solemn and seem to gaze into the distance.

At some point, *Pagla* would dress in new attire and suddenly approach the south side of the Mother's statue. There, he would quickly touch the palm of the Mother's right hand—his actions subtle and swift, indifferent to whether he was observed. He then briskly exited the temple and joined the crowd awaiting to carry the water-filled 'welfare pitcher' to the riverbank.

Surrounded by the crowd, they would set forth, with a selected individual—often Jiban Krishna Saha, a robust, fair-complexioned young man of considerable height—bearing the pitcher upon his head to collect the water. Although Jiban Krishna was not a childhood friend of *Bhaba Pagla,* he later became a devoted follower.

Following the collection of the water, *Pagla* would apply red 'sindoor' powder to the pitcher as part of the idol decoration and then place it at the feet of the Mother's statue. This marked the commencement of the festival. During the second phase, preparations for the Puja (worship) and the cooking of the holy meal began with grandeur.

Fruits were cut for 'prasad' (offerings), and there was a meticulous collection of incense powder, flowers, and 'Bilva Patra' (leaves of the stone-apple tree) for the worship. As the evening approached, *Pagla* would begin his dance, swirling two burning 'mosambi' oranges tied to strings, immersing himself in the oration and vibrancy of the sacred ceremony.

****

CHAPTER 7

The Hindu Festival (The worship by dancing)

The atmosphere was electric with over fifty hand-drum players and several 'Shehnai' musicians creating a symphony. The air was filled with the crowd's chants of 'Jai *Bhaba Pagla*' and 'Jai Maa.' The festivities reached a climax as *Bhaba Pagla* danced, waving various objects—burning incense sticks, one hundred eight earthen lamps, a large conch, a piece of cloth or handkerchief, a plate of flowers, and a 'chamar' (a fly-whisk fan made from yak tail or wool). As the 'Arati' concluded, holy water was sprinkled from a conch upon the devotees' heads as a blessing of peace. This was followed by *Bhaba Pagla* offering a holy meal to Goddess Kali. Instead of animal sacrifices, an offering of fruits and vegetables was presented, reinforcing *Pagla's* non-violent approach to worship.

This non-violent practice was consistent throughout the temples established by *Bhaba Pagla.* Animal sacrifices were eschewed in honour of the Goddess, a testament to his commitment to compassionate reverence.

During one significant worship service of Goddess Kali, the author of the book, Param Guru *Bhaba Pagla,* was present. He shared his observations of *Pagla,* who was dressed in crimson, wrapped in a blue cloth, and adorned with a garland of flowers, his face alight with joy. To prevent the eager crowd from encroaching too closely, a human chain was formed around *Pagla.* In a surprising moment, *Pagla* approached the author and quietly confessed, "I don't worship." This revelation puzzled the author, who had taken to heart the permission *Pagla* once granted him to pen his biography, with the caveat to refrain from embellishment, as it could cause *Pagla* to shrink with shyness.

Reflecting on this, the author recalled the words of a scholar, Partap Narayan, who recited in rhythm, "Welcome, Welcome, Welcome Her. As an honoured bride is welcomed." Whether *Bhaba Pagla* only offered welcome or not was a question that lingered in the author's mind.

In his later years, *Bhaba Pagla* spoke on 'Arati' (Prayer), suggesting that external items like incense sticks, Chamars, conch sounds, bells, or beating copper disks were unnecessary. He believed that 'Arati' should be a continuous inner act, with a song to reflect it: "I do 'Arati' of Shyama Maa every day. None of the ordinary trappings are needed—not a conch, bell, nor external light. The incense stick of faith is ever burning. My hair itself composes the chamar, and five earthen lamps representing the elements—earth, water, fire, air, and sky—are ceaselessly alight. The gentle ringing of my 'Brahma Bell' invites one into the full pleasure of being the Mother's child, filled with joy. My two conches sing an eternal current of love."

In the unique and non-violent tradition established by *Bhaba Pagla,* the ritual sacrifice involved offering fruits serially: 1) Ginger, 2) Banana, 3) Cucumber, 4) Sugar cane, and 5) Ash gourd. Each fruit was symbolically bisected with a large chopper, a beautiful yet benign substitute for the violent animal sacrifices of the past. This was carried out by a designated person under *Pagla's* directive, who would perform the symbolic gestures of sacrifice. This individual was draped in new cloth and adorned with a round mark made of red 'Sindoor' powder on his forehead, bestowed by *Pagla* himself.

The man's eyes would widen, reflecting a depth of thoughtfulness as he received a large 'kharga' (a special large chopper) from *Pagla,* who then escorted him to the sacrificial altar.

Meanwhile, *Pagla* entered the temple of Goddess Kali, leaving an open space from the temple's door to the sacrificial spot, flanked by onlookers arranged in long rows.

Pagla would look at the statue of Kali and signal to the performer to begin the sacrifices of Ginger, Banana, Sugar cane, Cucumber, and finally, thirteen Ash gourds—one by one. This procedure was replicated during every annual function across the many temples founded by *Bhaba Pagla.*

At the conclusion of the sacrifices, *Pagla* would usher the individual back to the temple, where his outfit was changed. Through these rituals—filling the Mangal Ghat (Pitcher of welfare) with water, dancing with the waving lamp, offering the 'Bhog' (holy meal), and sacrificing fruits—*Pagla's* worship of the Almighty Mother was completed in four ceremonial stages, typically concluding around 8 to 8:30 p.m.

Post-ceremony, music and songs dedicated to the Almighty Mother would resonate, drawing in thousands of watchers, devotees, and disciples. Following the performances, 'prasada' (the Holy Meal) was shared among those seated on the ground in rows, bordered by decorated cloths and canvas sheets. The crowd would gaze upon *Pagla,* with many bowing in reverence or presenting gifts for worship.

Pagla would offer a single acknowledging glance to the multitude but remembered everyone distinctly. This was evident in the case of a sub-Inspector of Police from Dhamrai, named Mohammad, who hailed from Barishal district and followed Islam. One evening, he came to *Pagla,* greeting him with, "I have come, Baba (Father)," but soon after, he disappeared.

The next morning, *Pagla* dispatched a search party for Mohammad. After some effort, he was found lying on his side. Upon hearing *Pagla's* name, Mohammad quickly rose, rubbing his eyes, and presented himself to *Pagla.* To *Pagla's* inquiry about his whereabouts the previous night, Mohammad responded with a bowed head, silent, like one acknowledging wrongdoing.

Bhaba Pagla, seized by inspiration, swiftly took up a pen and paper to compose a poem, which was his customary practice. Upon finishing, he handed the freshly penned song to a devotee and instructed, "Read it aloud, for I am hard of hearing." This request was not unusual for *Pagla*, who often claimed difficulty in hearing as a way to encourage loud recitations.

The song was read with vigor:

"Brother, why commit sins beyond measure? Do not forfeit your destiny by earning curses. Maintain restraint in all your actions, Observe quietly with watchful eyes. Stay silent yet know there is one who oversees; Never forget Him, for He is weighing you, hear this, seasoned sir.

When you partake in secretive deeds, know that He is watching from within your own heart, Why else would it tremble with such feeling? In this darkest of ages, 'Kali Yuga', all seems to decline."

As the song echoed, tears dampened the steps where *Bhaba Pagla* stood, recalling a tale of another Muslim devotee, Khurshed Ali Chowdhury. A stout man always seen with a smile, Khurshed hailed from Noakhali and worked as a Hakim in the subdivision of Mymensingh district. Having learned about *Bhaba Pagla* while in Manikganj and Tangile, he sought him out and, upon finding *Pagla*, became utterly devoted to him.

Blending seamlessly into *Pagla's* life, Khurshed would seize every chance to visit Aamta and spend time with *Pagla*, who never differentiated people based on caste or creed, embracing everyone as his own. On one occasion, *Pagla* entered Khurshed's office at the S.D.O. court, greeting him with "I have come, my son." Overjoyed and surprised, Khurshed exclaimed, "Come, *Pagla*! How fortunate am I?" His entrance caused quite a stir in the court.

Amidst the commotion, Khurshed, flustered, struggled to find a suitable place for *Bhaba Pagla* to sit. *Pagla* accepted the offer to take a seat on a chair, bringing a crowd to Khurshed's office. In a moment of exuberance, Khurshed addressed the crowd, "Everyone here listens to me, Father." *Pagla* probed, "My son, what is it that does not listen to anyone?" Pondering his words, those present in the room fell into deep thought until Khurshed, at last, invited *Pagla* to share his insight.

In response, *Pagla* requested, "Well, give me a piece of paper and a pen." A pen and paper were promptly provided. *Pagla* then composed another poem:

"Death does not listen to anyone, Lurking, it strikes at any moment. Mahamaya (Goddess) entices with her embrace, Weaving a subtle net of mortality.

Every man decries, 'None of mine remain!' Yet being alive is a marvel in itself, there is no room for complacency. With a modicum of patience, unending riches could be yours.

Remember, mortality is our shared fate. To live longer, learn the virtue of truth, for in truth lies the knowledge of life's end. Life and death are in your hands – *Bhaba Pagla* speaks this truth.

Chant his name with reverence, and untimely death you'll eschew."

Khurshed, with tears welling in his eyes at the first line, read the song aloud, each word weighed with deep contemplation.

Such was the essence of *Bhaba Pagla*, treasured by all for his profound wisdom and compassion, a figure beyond compares. Similar affection was held for another, Aziz Miya, a resident of Aautpara village in the Manikganj subdivision, presently in Bangladesh, yet another soul touched by the grace of *Bhaba Pagla.*

Aziz Miya, who was a classmate of *Bhaba Pagla* at Pakutiya school, had fair skin and the contemplative nature of a Vaishnava—

a devotee of Krishna. He was known for his religious disposition, surrounded by many Tulsi plants (holy basil), which led people to refer to him as Sadhu.

Aziz Miya would often communicate with *Bhaba Pagla* and held a firm respect for him. Aziz had learned some techniques of Hata Yoga, claiming he had acquired certain powers. Sometimes he would boast about these to *Pagla. Bhaba Pagla,* in response, would comment that such learning was a matter of "two pices," questioning, "What will you do with that?"

One day, the limitations of Aziz's Hata Yoga became apparent during an incident at the bank of the Sitalakhya river. As *Bhaba Pagla* and Aziz Sadhu prepared to cross the river, Aziz proclaimed, "I will walk on the water's surface."

Bhaba Pagla simply said, "Is it so? Then go ahead."

Aziz inquired, "And what will you do?"

Bhaba Pagla replied, "I will observe—do whatever you intend to do."

When Aziz stepped into the water, his legs immediately sank. *Bhaba Pagla* told him, "You will not be able to cross the river in this way. Come, follow me."

In that moment, *Bhaba Pagla* remembered his goddess, Kali, to whom he devoted worship. The Almighty Mother took pity on him and miraculously made a way by dividing the water of the Sitalakhya, enabling them to cross the river without difficulty, while Aziz followed, humbled by his inability.

The life story of *Bhaba Pagla* demonstrates that his capabilities extended beyond crossing water; he triumphed over water, land, and sky. One morning, *Bhabendra* and Debendra were digging a pit for a toilet on the east side of the temple in the house of Aamta. *Bhaben*dra, wearied from the laborious digging, was then joined by their mother, Gayasundari, who stood nearby.

Observing their fatigue, she offered, "Give me the basket, and I will help throw out the heaps of soil." Encouraged by her support, both brothers continued their work, skipping their bath and dinner without notice.

However, they were startled by Gayasundari's voice coming from inside the house, scolding, "What are you doing, forgetting to take a bath and have dinner?"

Both *Bhabendra* and Debendra looked at each other, bewildered. Debendra finally spoke up, "Mother, were you not just outside helping us with the soil a moment ago?"

Gayasundari, perplexed, replied, "Have you gone mad? When did I come out to lift the soil?"

This experience hints at the mysterious influence of *Bhaba Pagla's* spiritual presence, appearing to transcend the ordinary limits of time and place.

*Bhaben*dra's eyes filled with tears as he came to the realization that the Almighty Mother had appeared in the guise of his mother. *Bhaba Pagla,* reflecting on these profound events, composed an essay highlighting incidences of divine intervention in the lives of great worshippers:

For ages, Khayapa Beti (Almighty Mother), in her youthful exuberance, plays upon the chest of Mahadev, with many calling her as they wish.

In Birbhum, pups played during the worship of Bama Khayapa, making it seem as though the Almighty Mother awoke in a hut adorned with skulls.

In Halisahar, people wondered if the Almighty Mother would adorn the fence while her rhythmic songs of Ramprasad filled the air, and she, delighted, requested a devoted man to sing for her on the riverbank.

In Bardhaman, the two feet of Shyama (Almighty Mother) reside in the songs of Kamalakanta, who sought refuge at her feet when menaced by a demon.

In Kamarpukur, Shyama (Almighty Mother) was ever-present with Ramakrishna Paramhansa, often revealing herself to the disciple before the guru.

In Natore, the tale of Ramakrishna and the Almighty Mother was inscribed in the heart, with Divine Mother personally addressing Ramakrishna with affectionate calls.

In Meher, Sarbahanda Adhikary and his assistant, Punadaa, revered Shankari (the Goddess) who was believed to have awaken in the crematorium, embodying the cycle of rebirth.

In Pabna, Rajkrishna Sah, a devotee of Kirtikhola, surrendered to the Mother, and his Guru, despite indulging in liquor, glimpsed nectar in the Holy Meal of the Almighty Mother.

In Comilla, Manmohan and Arta Uddin kept the name of the Almighty Mother always on their lips, blending their labour with divine invocation, leading to the belief that the Mother with three eyes (trinayani) had become a part of their existence.

And in the village of Aamta, amidst the singing of songs dedicated to *Bhaba Pagla*, the Almighty Mother was rumoured to aid devotees by carrying soil during the day, not just at night.

Bhaba Pagla was also deft at embroidery, often saying in jest, "All subjects except for *Bhaba Pagla.*" He embroidered a likeness of Gandhi on fabric, which was widely admired. Women from the area would come to him to learn needlework, which he taught near the Kali temple.

Among his students was Renu Chanda, a doctor's daughter, known for her beauty and impetuousness. She would often speak without reserve, once remarking, "You work with such harbour (haste)." *Bhaba Pagla* humorously replied, "I am in harbour to grant you a husband like Har (another name of Shiva)."

Renu, failing to grasp the depth of *Bhaba Pagla's* wisdom, once offensively remarked as *Pagla* was anointing a statue of Kali, "The girl you care for is so dark-skinned." *Pagla,* in response to her comment, composed a soulful song celebrating the dark-skinned daughter of creation:

"A dark-skinned girl, with a radiance that lights the cosmos, my dark-skinned girl wed Shiva, and having birthed many, she rests again upon Shiva's chest. The Divine Mother is the maiden with free-flowing hair, Her nails like lotuses bearing the sun and moon. Sages meditate upon her, seeking her essence but finding no end. I am Kali, you are Kali; the universe itself is a grand Kali."

Pagla's poetic response expressed the incomparable beauty and power of the dark-skinned goddess and the divine presence within us all.

The sky and the wind are all manifestations of Kali, leading people to invoke her by saying 'Kali.' *Bhaba Pagla* conveyed that those who contemplate Kali will be eternally joyful, even at the time of death, causing the deity of death to turn away. With this declaration, *Pagla* took his leave.

One day, a forty-year-old man arrived at the temple, shouting to find *Bhaba Pagla,* wondering where his Kali was and if everyone was asleep. *Pagla,* who was in a small room beside the temple, came out at the sound of the shouting. With his usual approach to newcomers, he asked the man, "What is your name, my son? Where are you from? Have you come to see me? Who told you about me?"

The man replied affirmatively, mentioning that he heard about *Pagla* from the magician P.C. Sarkar, to whom he was related as a maternal uncle. He had likened *Bhaba Pagla's* powers to magic tricks and was curious to meet this 'sudden saint' and see if *Pagla's* Kali was asleep.

Pagla composed a song in response to the man's implied challenge rather than addressing the provocations directly. Gazing upon the image of Kali Maa Anandamoyee, *Pagla* quickly wrote a song elucidating that the goddess does not sleep and that if she doesn't seem to respond, it's because she is playfully unwary.

Pagla handed the newcomer the paper with the song and asked him to read it aloud, citing his purported difficulty hearing as a reason, a familiar aspect of his demeanor. The song *Pagla* wrote was both an answer for the visitor and a broader message about the time-flowing ceaselessly:

"If you call, the Mother (Almighty) will respond—Kali (the goddess) does not sleep. If after calling, the Mother remains silent, consider it her playful mood. She resides within the entirety of the universe, eternally awake as 'Brahmamoyee Kali.' I have yet to learn how to call her sincerely—that's why the Mother laughs heartily.

I have called her 'Mother' over the days gone by." As the newcomer read the piece, *Pagla* reminded him that the Mother is the universal creatress and the ultimate force behind creation, preservation, and destruction. He urged that she would surely respond if called sincerely, even a soft call with a little devotion can lead to many unfolding events, which are described in the subsequent pages.

There were three gardens filled with flowers surrounding the temple of Kali, where 'Jaba' flowers held a special significance for *Bhaba Pagla.* He mentioned 'Jaba' flowers in his songs, and they had a special place within the gardens. Fifty-two varieties of 'Jaba' flowers blossomed there; each species labelled with its name. Some of the *Jaba* flowers were named *Ambika, Alakananda, Anandamoyee, Indrani, Katyayani, Gayatri, Gouri, Chandika, Chandranana,*

Jagadhatri, Devabala, Nilkanti, Panchamukhi, Fullara, Brahmamoyee, Raktaranga, among others, creating a vivid and beautiful display.

Bhaba Pagla, a revered saint in India, was renowned for his teachings which often emphasized that through devotion, the seemingly impossible could be achieved. He would often narrate stories, echoing a powerful message: "Your devotion should not be less." He wholly believed that devotion surpassed all, even surpassing the wisdom of sages. *Bhaba Pagla* sang of a world where divine love and affection were paramount, and devotees would be carried by its current.

The esteemed saint was known for his relentless travels from one village to another, fuelled by his affection for the people. In one such instance, the villagers of a Manikganj subdivision eagerly wished to join him at a festival, yet circumstances never allowed it. During this period, they hatched a plan inspired by Jiban Krishna Saha, a man of considerable stature with a height of around six feet and an impressive strength. Jiban Krishna had a fair complexion, spoke eloquently, and shared *Bhaba Pagla's* preference for a humble and simple lifestyle, shunning lavish comforts in favour of simplicity.

As part of their plan to bring *Bhaba Pagla* to their village festival, the villagers conspired to have Jiban Krishna carry the saint away by breaking through a bamboo fence at night. Despite the plan's secrecy, Jiban Krishna, aware of *Bhaba Pagla's* extraordinary will power, disclosed their intentions. "They plan to take you to their village tonight, and I will carry you. Please make it easy for me," he pleaded. To his amazement, when he lifted *Bhaba Pagla,* he felt as light as a piece of cork—testament to the saint's grace and a task that would have been impossible otherwise.

An intriguing incident took place in Faridpur, Bangladesh, involving *Bhaba Pagla* and his devotees. After a soulful singing session, the devotees wished to move him upstairs in a wealthy man's double-storey cement house. When a robust Muslim man—

with pride in his considerable strength—attempted to lift the saint, he found him astonishingly heavy. Despite his muscular 42-inch chest, he could barely take a step before his chest bone strained under the weight, compelling him to concede and set *Bhaba Pagla* down. The incident served as a lesson to shed ego to truly understand and embrace the saint's teaching.

The narrative then shifts to Dinesh Chatterjee, an infamous, fearless dacoit known for his intelligence and brazen approaches in the Manikganj subdivision. Daringly robbing rich households after openly announcing his intentions, Dinesh maintained a peculiar honour code, especially towards women whom he neither disrespected nor tyrannized. Even such a man once requested *Bhaba Pagla* to visit his home. Accepting the invitation, *Bhaba Pagla* arrived with his entourage to be affectionately greeted by Dinesh as "Father." It was a poignant reunion as tears filled Dinesh's eyes upon hearing *Bhaba Pagla's* arrival.

Their exchange was a significant moment. Dinesh, filled with anxiousness, inquired about his fate. *Bhaba Pagla* reassured him with the words, "What is there to fear when I am behind you?" This affirmation served as a source of encouragement, transforming a sense of helplessness into courage—a rare gift that *Bhaba Pagla* bestowed upon many.

By assuring Dinesh and others in need, *Bhaba Pagla* stood as a beacon of hope and strength, epitomizing the empowering essence of spiritual guidance upon those who followed him. His life and actions continued to inspire, leaving an indelible impact on those fortunate enough to have crossed his path.

Bhaba Pagla was known for his soul-stirring songs and the profound stories he would share in a tender, affectionate voice. One day, as he played the harmonium, he gently addressed Dinesh, the notorious dacoit, saying, "My son, why overthink? Observe how I too 'steal' from the Divine Mother."

He drew a parallel between Dinesh's acts of dacoity, where Dinesh would ask, "Mother, give me your key. Give me some ornaments. Give me gold," and his own spiritual requests, highlighting that sages and monks would petition the Mother Goddess Chandi for beauty and wealth. However, *Bhaba Pagla* considered these desires foolish. "Why should I seek wealth and jewels when I can have the Mother entirely? By desiring the Mother in her entirety, all else follows," he explained. "So, you too should call out to the Mother earnestly – that is my form of 'dacoity'."

At these words, Dinesh wept, as if his tainted mind was being purified by *Pagla's* wisdom. *Bhaba Pagla* approached Dinesh, holding his golden stick, and with a symbolic gesture, placed his foot upon Dinesh's chest, signifying the removal of Dinesh's desires and attachments.

After leaving Dinesh appeased in every possible way, *Bhaba Pagla* returned to Aamta. Curious about the dacoit's fate, *Pagla* inquired, "What has become of Dinesh?" The response came that Dinesh had abandoned his life of crime. While people mocked his change of heart, speculating that he roamed his house at night out of habit, *Bhaba Pagla* knew better. "By invoking the Mother, one finds peace," he assured. "The Divine Mother will surely show him compassion."

Despite *Bhaba Pagla's* compassionate and peaceful nature, there were some who harboured jealousy and malice towards him, concocting lies and even plotting his death. On one occasion, a group of young men invited him to their village for a festival. Under the veil of night, they deceptively mixed tobacco powder and poison with molasses in a drink, which they offered to *Bhaba Pagla.* He consumed the juice with innocent trust. While the poison did harm his vocal cords, making his voice hoarse, it did not take his life, and the young men's nefarious plan to kill him failed.

One day, *Bhaba Pagla* faced a confrontation when Radhegovinda, a military man, accosted him under a tree away from the path. The situation escalated quickly as Radhegovinda, in a fit of temper, drew his revolver and threatened to shoot the saint. Unfazed, *Bhaba Pagla* wryly responded, "Oh, you want to shoot me? You may not realize that I have my own 'revolver'. You have a gun with six bullets, but mine is far greater, with countless bullets. Can you really take me on?" Despite this warning, Radhegovinda, unable to contain his rage, discharged all six bullets at *Bhaba Pagla*, none of which struck the saint.

Radhegovinda was astounded, especially when he claimed to see multiple images of *Bhaba Pagla* surrounding the tree, making it impossible for him to discern which was the true *Bhaba Pagla.* As the gun fell silent, having expended its ammunition, *Bhaba Pagla* laughed heartily and said to Radhegovinda, "I stand here beside you. If I chose to punish you, you would be defenseless. Haven't you heard that *Bhaba Pagla* is a living ('Taja') saint? And if you invert 'Taja', it becomes 'Jata' (a bad thing), which I can turn you into. Why harbour such malice? Leave at once." Ashamed, Radhegovinda left, bowing his head in defeat.

Meanwhile, at the Kali temple in Aamta, an unrelated incident unfolded. Ganga Charan Saha, who had brought a statue made of black stone from Kolkata, also brought a beautiful woman to reside in his village home. She was a young lady, radiant and adorned with a bold red 'bindi' on her forehead. However, Saha's wife grew suspicious and fearful of the mysterious arrival. Consumed by dread and suspecting her husband's fidelity, she turned her thoughts to *Bhaba Pagla* for solace, remembering, "What is there to fear? *Bhaba Pagla* provides refuge to those in turmoil."

Without delay, she sought *Bhaba Pagla's* help, bringing the young woman with her to the temple. She expressed her unease, wishing to entrust the stranger to his care, saying, "I wish to leave this girl with you. Do as you see fit." Perceiving the wife's anxiety,

Bhaba Pagla agreed and offered to let the young woman stay at the temple, nicknaming her 'Bhairabi Mother' due to her striking 'bindi'.

Bhaba Pagla, however, cautioned Bhairabi not to touch the revered Anandamoyee statue, instructing, "You can help with all other tasks but do not touch 'Maa' Anandamoyee." The village soon came to know her as Bhairabi 'Maa', and she served well in her new role at the temple.

But an unanticipated, or rather, a real event occurred in her life. One day, while cleaning near the Anandamoyee statue, Bhairabi, overwhelmed by a sudden impulse, reached out to clean the statue itself. As she bowed down and made contact with the statue, a girl seemed to emerge from it, seizing her shoulder with the intention to bite. Many might doubt such an occurrence, yet Bhairabi could not avoid the painful grip and screamed in agony, falling unconscious.

Alerted by her cries, *Bhaba Pagla* rushed to the temple, along with the household members gathering around. *Pagla* implored the Anandamoyee 'Maa' to release the girl. He then forcefully liberated Bhairabi from the statue's clutches. After some days, they managed to locate Bhairabi's grandmother's home in Nabadwip.

Years passed, and *Bhaba Pagla* eventually heard news about the young woman named Bhairabi. She had married and was living a content domestic life. On the 2nd of Bhadra in the Bengali year 1385—likely August 1978—*Bhaba Pagla* was immersed in the joyous spirit of a 'Kirtan' session one evening. During a brief pause, his attendant and follower, Shreeman Sathoy Chand, mentioned Bhairabi. *Pagla* recounted how Bhairabi had recently sought him out. Now aged, she had returned to show the devotees the healed scars where she had once been bitten.

"Is this wondrous play simply an unexpected incident?" the author muses. Another story begins with the Ghosh family of

Garparh in the Manikganj subdivision, who became devotees of *Bhaba Pagla* and would frequent the Kali temple at Aamta. When *Pagla* visited their home with his group, it became a celebration of song, inviting many from the village to join. Among them, Mohini Ghosh's daughter, known affectionately as Tulu, would sing with heartfelt emotion. Despite her young age and dark complexion, Tulu's voice was unparalleled in its devotion.

An incident occurred during one of these gatherings. As Tulu continued to sing, deeply engrossed in her performance, the end of her 'sari' slipped from her shoulder. Tulu, her hands busy playing the harmonium, did not notice. *Pagla,* however, saw something extraordinary: Two luminous arms appeared alongside Tulu's own, securing the 'sari' back over her shoulders. Wondering who could be this guardian angel, *Pagla* soon realised it was the grace of the Almighty Mother. He wept at the sight, and from that moment, Tulu earned his deep respect. He even composed a poem in her honour and preserved it at the Aamta temple.

Yet another episode unfolds as *Bhaba Pagla* served as a watchman during the Durga Puja festival at Gajendra Mohan's house in Aamta, where gold and silver utensils adorned the worship altar. When Purna Chakraborty, the main priest, fell ill with cholera during a terrible storm, it was left to *Bhaba Pagla* to ensure his safe transport to Baliati. With trusty boatman Mohar at the helm, they set out by boat.

On their journey, amidst the bustling Saturiya market, a tragic sight startled them: a young girl, adorned with jewellery, was floating lifelessly in the water. Mohar exclaimed in despair, thinking her dead. *Bhaba Pagla,* after verifying the girl was indeed about seven years old, instructed Mohar to bring her aboard and onto the shore.

Crowds gathered as the girl's anxious parents arrived. *Pagla* commanded that no one, not even her mother, should touch her just yet. He asked the villagers to bring *conch shells* and *kasar* (*a* discs to create sound). With an air of solemnity, *Pagla* touched the girl's forehead with two fingers at the brow centre. Miraculously, the girl's eyes opened, and she returned to consciousness. Her parents profusely thanked *Bhaba Pagla,* who in turn asked only to be invited to her wedding in the future. As the girl grew up and eventually married, it remains unknown whether the invitation to *Pagla* was ever extended.

****

CHAPTER 8

Familial Milestones and Divine Encounters

As time passed, *Bhaben*, along with his brother, grew older, eventually reaching the age of 26. Despite this, neither of them had been married, and the absence of the family patriarch amplified the burden of responsibility. With the weight of caring for her two sons resting heavily on her shoulders, their mother sought affirmation from *Bhaben* regarding his marriage. Directly, and without any prior discussion, she approached her son with a plea, expressing her deep concern about his unmarried status. She voiced her poignant plea, desperately urging *Bhaben* to fulfil her wish, emphasizing the impact it had on her well-being since the departure of their father. Feeling the weight of the responsibility and the emotional plea from his mother, *Bhaben* acknowledged his agreement, understanding the impact his decision had on her peace of mind in the future. He was, however, also resolute in his conditions, conveying the imperative timeline for the marriage arrangements. As *Bhaben* conveyed his decision, his mother, gratified and reassured, swiftly turned her focus to making the necessary preparations for the imminent marriage. A prospective bride had already been chosen for *Bhaben* from the village of Jamurki, named Shaibalini, daughter of Basanta Babu and similar arrangements were made for Devendra Mohan, with Renu Bala, the daughter of Jyotindra Nath Saha, from the village of Amta, chosen as his prospective bride. The pending marriage was set for the 26th of Shraban in the Bengali month, and decisive and meticulous efforts were made to secure the agreement of both the prospective brides' families, culminating in the confirmation of the marriage arrangements.

As the day of the 26th of Shraban (12th August as per English Calendar) approached, only a few days remained, the mother informed Girin, *Bhaben*'s elder brother, of the impending marriage, urging him to bring his wife for the occasion. She sought reassurance from Girin, desiring his consent to confidently make all the necessary arrangements and after a moment of deep contemplation, blessed without entering any debate.

His mother, preoccupied with the multitude of tasks entailed by her sons' imminent marriages, busied herself with the preparations, gradually drawing the attention of relatives and neighbours to participate in the extraordinary event. Meanwhile, *Bhaba Pagla's* thoughts turned towards the enigmatic play of the Almighty Mother, pondering over her involvement in the forthcoming domestic affairs. Amidst the unfolding preparations and discussions, *Bhaben,* in accordance with the custom of the village, partook in the rituals of the Hindu marriage ceremony, symbolically engaging in the traditions and customs. However, amidst the ceremonies, his thoughts drifted to the mysterious and miraculous voice known to him since childhood, signifying an encounter with the divine. Seeing a signal from the Almighty Mother on how to cut the banana leaf with a knife, *Bhaben* perceived the profound guidance in the mirror of his wisdom.

The conclusion of the marriage ceremony was marked by *Bhabendra* Mohan's symbolic act of slicing the banana leaf into seven pieces, followed by the disappearance of the almighty Mother. This mysterious play of the almighty Mother left a profound impact, as her fleeting presence went unnoticed by all. *Bhaba Pagla* accepted his wife after the marriage, and he continued his routine of spending his days and nights in the temple, finding solace in poetry, songs, and blessing the devotees seeking the almighty Mother's divine grace. Despite his spiritual commitments, he appeared careless about his domestic responsibilities, prompting curiosity and reflections among his childhood friends about his future and the potential impact of marriage on his spiritual path. The birth of *Bhaba Pagla's* son, Sanat, and daughter, Pratima, brought significant joy to the family, while a memorable incident involving Pratima, and the red scarf (saari) added a touch of wonder and bemusement.

The incidents interwoven with his domestic responsibilities and spiritual pursuits offered a glimpse into the complexities and spiritual essence that defined *Bhaba Pagla's* family life.

Bhaben's dedication to the temple consumed his days and nights, with the temple room serving as a place for both rest and continued spiritual expression. His unwavering commitment to writing poems and singing songs persisted, attracting devotees seeking the blessings of the almighty Mother. Alongside these spiritual endeavors, *Bhaben* diligently visited the villagers, ensuring their well-being and providing support in various ways. These efforts were punctuated by continued incidents of blessings and miracles attributed to the almighty Mother, reinforcing the spiritual essence surrounding *Bhaben.*

The contrast between *Bhaben*'s spiritual focus and his relative indifference to domestic responsibilities stirred curiosity among his childhood friends. This led to discussions about the potential future trajectory of his life, drawing parallels to the exploits of great men described in the Veda Purana, including Buddha, Sri Chaitanya, and the story of Rama Krishna's marriage. The contemplation also delved into the potential impact of marriage on *Bhaben*'s spiritual path, prompting deliberations on the path he might follow.

A significant development in *Bhaba Pagla's* domestic life was marked by the birth of his first son, Sanat, and his daughter,

Pratima. This event underscored the evolving dynamics of his family life.

When Pratima, at the tender age of three, encountered a traveling salesman who had come to their home to sell sarees, a significant incident unfolded. Among the displayed items was a red saree that caught Pratima's attention, prompting her to take it and walk beside the statue of Anandamoyee Ma. Unexpectedly, Anandamoyee - *Brahmamoyee Maa* gripped the saree so tightly that Pratima couldn't retrieve it, leading to her distress and tears. Upon hearing her cries, Shaibalini rushed to the temple and attempted to release the saree from the grip of the almighty Mother, but to no avail. In a pivotal moment, *Bhaba Pagla* was summoned, and amidst Shaibalini's plea to retrieve the saree for Pratima, he acknowledged the significance of the situation. In a poignant declaration, he shared his belief that the one who could successfully retrieve the saree would be its rightful owner. This led to the agreement to retrieve the saree, and it was then carefully folded and placed inside a glass Almeriah within the temple, where it remains observed to this day.

This retelling seeks to elucidate the significant impact of the encounter with the almighty Mother, highlighting the reverence and thoughtful consideration in handling the saree within the temple.

The birth of *Bhaba Pagla's* third child, a son named Sankalpa, symbolized the promises of their familial desires, with each of the three children representing different types of desire - passion, anger, and illusion, alluding to the name of their youngest son, Sankalpa. These events highlighted the intricate balance between spiritual devotion and the responsibilities of domestic life experienced by *Bhaba Pagla* and his family.

Additionally, a poignant moment where *Bhaba Pagla* adorned the temple with blue flowers offered a glimpse into the ongoing spiritual journey and domestic milestones in his life, reflecting a deep connection to the sacred space and the spiritual essence that defined their family's experiences.

Tragic Loss and Rituals for Mother's Departure A solemn and unexpected turn of events occurred during a function at No. 4 Sova Bazar when the news of the passing of Gayasundari Devi, *Bhaba Pagla's* mother, surfaced. It was revealed that she had consciously foreseen her death, forbidding her family from informing *Bhaba Pagla,* as she did not wish to delay her departure. Following her passing, the brothers, Girindra Mohan, Deben, and *Bhaben,* renowned for their devotion to their mother, performed rituals for her peaceful passage.

Significance of the Pindo Dan Ritual *Bhaba Pagla,* in a poignant display of love and respect, composed a heartfelt poem inscribed at the cremation site of his mother in Amta Kali Bari in Dhaka, marking a touching tribute to the cherished bond between a mother and her son. While reflecting on the inevitability of mortality and the illusions of life, *Bhaba Pagla's* poignant words encompassed the profound truths about life and death. The poignant narrative further revealed the brothers' solemn commitment and *Bhaba Pagla's* profound spiritual realization, epitomizing the depth of their understanding and meaningful connections.

If there are any specific details or sentiments you would like to further explore or any adjustments you'd like to propose, please feel free to let me know!

****

CHAPTER 9

The Golden Stick

The story of *Bhaba Pagla's* golden stick is woven into the fabric of his life as an enduring memory among his miraculous tales. The origin of this golden stick dates back to a time near Aamta Village, six to seven miles from a hill that marked the border between the Dhaka district and the Tangile subdivision of the Mymensingh District.

Bhaba Pagla was traversing a bamboo forest alongside the Banshai river when he was accompanied by his house servant, Ganesh Biswas. As they walked, a thin strand of bamboo brushed against *Bhaba Pagla.* He took note of it, regarding the plant with a discerning eye. The bamboo touched him again, prompting an internal dialogue with himself. *Pagla* was reminded of 'Trailanga Swami', a revered figure, and decided to confront what he perceived as the bamboo's obstinate character.

Using a Nepalese *Kukri* (a kind of knife that), Ganesh had strapped to his waist, *Bhaba Pagla* took the implement and cut the bamboo thirteen times until it was severed. When questioned about the significance of the thirteen chops, *Bhaba Pagla* replied with a play on words, suggesting the cuts were meant to break through the bamboo's defiant nature.

Insisting that they take the piece with them, Ganesh viewed it as nothing more than a trivial fragment, but to *Bhaba Pagla,* it was far more than that. Upon returning to the temple, *Pagla* found inspiration in the bamboo and wrote a poem reflecting on its various historic and mythic roles: as a vessel for plucking 'Jaba' flowers for the deity, as the bow of Lord Rama in the Treta Yuga, as Krishna's flute in the Dwapara Yuga, and even as an implement used by Harischandra in a crematorium—all illustrations of the bamboo's significance across different ages.

Back home, *Bhaba Pagla* dedicated himself to the crafting of the bamboo piece. He transformed it into a stick over five feet long, meticulously shaping and smoothing it until it met his standards. The tip of the stick was then wrapped in a sheet of rolled silver, and each node was adorned with a golden sheath. Etched upon these sheets were symbols of auspiciousness and spirituality: the welfare wheel, the conch, the temple heart surrounded by a thousand lotuses, the *Kurma* (tortoise), *Meen* (fish), the coiled Kundalini serpent energy, and the design of a Mosque—each a significant representation of the divine and the universal pursuit of spiritual enlightenment.

The bamboo stick, which *Bhaba Pagla* had carefully crafted, was further embellished with pearls and jewels set along its length. In a moment suffused with sanctity, the stick was blessed by the touch of Anandamoyee, the Mother of the Universe, and infused with the will power of *Bhaba Pagla* himself. This consecration endowed the stick with spiritual potency, and it was said to possess the miraculous ability to return of its own volition if lost in the river Ganga or if it was stolen.

The golden stick was also reputed to have healing powers; it could revive the dying, grant joy and offspring to childless couples, and cure those afflicted with diseases like tuberculosis and leprosy. Decoits and ruffians, upon its touch, would transform into sages. The stick in the hand of *Bhaba Pagla* was not just a symbol but a conduit of immense virtue and power, and the sight of it became synonymous with the saint himself.

On one day, in the village of Jhitka within the Manikganj Subdivision, an incident demonstrated the power of this golden stick. While walking with his group of followers, *Bhaba Pagla* altered his usual route. Curious, one devotee questioned the change, to which *Pagla* replied, "Let us explore this path," leading the way. Shortly after, they encountered a Muslim man, Nizamuddin, who was inconsolable and suffering from leprosy.

As Nizamuddin sat beneath a tree, crying for divine intervention, *Bhaba Pagla* approached him, holding his golden stick. The man's condition was severe, as he revealed that his disease had caused even his wife to expel him from their home. In a display of compassion, *Pagla* tapped him once with the stick and instructed him to eat a *martaman kala* (banana) after giving Nizamuddin a rupee to buy one. *Pagla* then continued on his journey, leaving behind a sentiment among his company that the day's walk had purposefully led to the salvation of Nizamuddin.

Years later, details emerged about Nizamuddin's fate after the encounter with *Bhaba Pagla*, who had left his birthplace of Aamta around 1950 during the tumultuous period of the Second World War and the partition of Bengal. *Pagla* established the temple of Maa *Bhaba*ni in Kalna, District Bardhaman, attracting new disciples and devotees. As he traveled, dispelling his sweet devotional songs of the Almighty Mother, crowds would gather around him, drawn by his growing reputation.

One such place frequented by *Bhaba Pagla* was the village of Sukhchar in the District of 24 Parganas, where the house of Thakur rested by the sacred Ganges—a site long considered hallowed for being a gathering place of Vaishnavism, the followers of Lord Krishna.

Over time, the land where Nityananda Prabhu had once held 'Kirtan' gatherings for the Vaishnavs was purchased by Mahendra Chattopadhyay, who constructed a house and a shrine for idol worship there. The statues of Maha Prabhu Sri Chaitanya and Nityananda that were installed there roughly two hundred and fifty years ago still stand to this day. The estate eventually came under the ownership of Jasoda Devi. As she aged, her eldest son,

Parimal Kumar Bandopadhyay, took responsibility for managing the property.

Jasoda Devi's family, including her sons Parimal Kumar and Bimal Kumar, their wives, and their children, held *Bhaba Pagla* in high regard and later became his disciples. Whenever he visited their home, the family ensured his comfort and attentively welcomed the devotees and disciples who accompanied him.

It was November 18th, 1968, corresponding to the 2nd Agrahayan in the Bengali Calendar year of 1375, when *Bhaba Pagla* had arrived at their home a few days earlier. As he prepared to return to Kalna, devotees gathered on the long courtyard by the Ganga River to pay their respects by touching his feet. Meanwhile, Shreemoti Chinmoyee Dey and Parimal Babu's daughter, Gopa, were trying to tune a song on the harmonium that *Bhaba Pagla* had composed in his youth.

At that moment, two young newcomers entered the house. They lay on the ground in a gesture of deep respect to salute *Bhaba Pagla.* Their appearance, with hair pulled back into buns and wearing loose shirts akin to 'Dike Bout' style, caught the eye. Addressed by *Pagla*, the oldest of the two named Krishna revealed they were from Rasmoni Road and had been seeking *Bhaba Pagla* for years, recalling their attempt to find him in Aamta during their childhood.

Krishna reminisced about seeing *Pagla* as a young teen, sharing how back then, the extent of *Pagla's* followers was known only to him and God, as Hindus and Muslims alike adored him. Krishna jovially warned that if *Pagla* were to return to his home country, the people would be so overjoyed that they might not let him leave, half-joking that they might end his life if he refused to make them disciples.

The conversation soon turned to Nizamuddin of Jhitka, the man with leprosy whom *Pagla* had helped. Krishna updated that

Nizamuddin had recovered, prospered, built a double-storey cement house, and had since married two more wives, all while maintaining deep reverence for *Bhaba Pagla,* worshipping his photograph daily.

Pagla humbly attributed such transformations to the power of devotion and faith rather than his own merit, while Krishna leaned over to the author and quietly inquired about the whereabouts of *Bhaba Pagla's* golden stick, noting its absence.

I, the author, informed Haray Krishna that the golden stick was at the temple in Kalna. *Bhaba Pagla* was currently keeping a bamboo stick instead. Our conversation captured the attention of everyone present, as Haray Krishna's words held a captivating charm. He revealed to *Bhaba Pagla* that he had traveled to America and, before his departure, had searched extensively for *Pagla. Bhaba Pagla* inquired if Haray Krishna had gone with Purna Das Baul, to which he confirmed and mentioned they sang *Bhaba Pagla's* songs there.

Intrigued, *Bhaba Pagla* asked if the people in America listened to his songs. Haray Krishna explained that his song 'Bole ki Manush ke Sadhu Kora Jaay?' had been recorded and was popular in both America and England. He then sang this and other songs for everyone present, expressing a desire to learn more. *Bhaba Pagla* encouraged this eagerness: "Well, you learn."

As the visitation grew, so did the desire to touch the golden stick, believed to possess the ability to cure diseases and resolve problems. It attracted not only the devout but also the covetous eyes of dacoits and thieves, among them Ibrahim Soleman, who became aware of *Bhaba Pagla's* golden stick.

One day, as *Bhaba Pagla* was returning to Aamta from Ketharpur, walking through the meadows at a brisk pace, Ibrahim lay in wait in a vast field along the Dhaleshwari riverbank, armed and determined. Yet, as he confronted *Bhaba Pagla* with a sharpened dagger, he could not foresee the profound transformation awaiting him at that very moment.

Bhaba Pagla halted and faced Ibrahim, questioning his intentions and reminding him of his own revered status as *Taja Sadhu* and the reverse, *Jata*, signifying that he could turn the worst into something profound. When *Pagla* gestured with the golden stick, something remarkable occurred. Ibrahim's eyes, once filled with malice, brimmed with tears and, kneeling before *Pagla*, he begged for mercy, renouncing his past ways.

Fleeing to the banks of the Dhaleshwari River, Ibrahim discarded his weapons into the river's embrace. No one knew of his whereabouts until, after many years, it was discovered that the fierce dacoit had transformed into a saintly *Fakir*, a testament to the redemptive power *Bhaba Pagla* and the golden stick held.

Years later, an Inspector General of Police named Upananda Mukherjee became intrigued by *Bhaba Pagla's* golden stick. Facing a minor issue, this high-ranking official and initiated disciple pondered his Gurudev's predicament. Resolved to address the problem, he invited *Bhaba Pagla* to his government residence with sincere hospitality.

Upon *Pagla's* afternoon arrival, he found Upananda's Gurudev seated on an elevated cot. Contrary to *Bhaba Pagla's* preference for simplicity, he sat on the floor alongside his companions. *Pagla* addressed Upananda's guru with a smile and thought-provoking advice, encouraging him to sit on the ground to avoid the fear of falling and to be grounded like himself. During the visit, the golden stick's beauty in *Pagla's* hand was undeniable.

As they conversed, Upananda Mukherjee suggested to *Bhaba Pagla* that, considering the precious golden stick he carried, it might be wise to keep a revolver for protection, offering to arrange a license for it. *Pagla* responded with a smile, implying that he already possessed such a 'revolver'—one that had been licensed for ages. When Upananda pressed for more details, *Bhaba Pagla* cryptically spoke of not needing to search for material protection, suggesting that in the face of the Almighty's dazzling light, all earthly powers dim.

Through this exchange, *Bhaba Pagla* imparted a deeper understanding: those who have faith in the unseen do not rely on the illusions of the material world. Upananda learned that seeking protection through conventional means was futile for those who trust in divine providence.

To this day, the golden stick resides within the temple of *Maa Bhabani* in Kalna and continues to provide hope and healing to many. The stick not only offers solace but also appears to hold the ability to address injustice, reinforcing the significance of right action and virtue.

Moved by these events and a fact-seeking individual's inquiry, *Bhaba Pagla* penned a poem, which he presented as a gift, reflecting on the golden stick's purpose and presence:

"The golden stick endures though thorns may scar, A tool to reprimand acts unjust, not far. A fan of yak's tail, a bamboo staff akin, To Vedanta and Rigveda, their essence within.

No difference it sees between ruler and the ruled, In wisdom and ignorance alike it schooled. Though pride may blind, the golden sheath shines bright, In the forest, a goddess, a queen in sight.

Conveying divine messages through every grove, Instructing all to worship with love, The bamboo lineage, its home amidst the stand. The bow of Ram, pure existence grand.

Krishna's flute, *Bhaba's* stick in hand, The justice-bearing staffs of Gour's command. In Nadia's Kingdom, the truth they speak, upholding what's right, supporting the meek."

****

CHAPTER 10

Ram Prashad Maha Prashad
Great Holy Meal

A few years after his mother's passing, *Bhaba Pagla* was invited to Kolkata by some friends. He stayed at house number four on Shoba Bazar Street. In the evenings, a gathering would assemble for song functions led by *Bhaba Pagla*, and these events were always well-attended. One night, after a session that concluded at 11 PM, *Pagla* told his close acquaintances that he intended to visit a place the following morning and invited anyone interested to accompany him, asking them to arrive early.

Curious about the destination, his friends inquired, but *Pagla* simply responded that they would find out in due time and mentioned that the journey would begin at Sealdah Station. Excited by the prospect of travel, the friends agreed to join him, and plans were made to meet at Sealdah Station the next day.

Upon meeting at the station, *Pagla* provided his companions with money to buy tickets to Halisahar. The group realized that *Pagla* intended to visit the dwelling place of Ramprasad family. Those who joined *Pagla* on this journey included Bidhu Bhushan Chaudhary, Ganga Charan Saha, Nadiya Govinda Saha, Amar Govinda Saha, Mohan Chaudhary, Bidhu Bhushan Saha, Satish Saha, Jeevan Krishna Saha, Nikunja Banik, Surendra Banik, and Nibaran Banik, among others.

Arriving at Halisahar station, they found no available vehicles and opted to walk, despite not knowing the way. Nevertheless, they followed *Bhaba Pagla*, who led the way with a swift pace, walking barefooted and remaining somehow untouched by dust.

Following a winding path through the forest, the companions began to feel unsure, but *Pagla* reassured them of his presence. Suddenly, a jackal appeared from the forest and paced ahead of them; *Pagla* advised the group to follow the animal. The jackal disappeared after a while, and then a strikingly white cow with a bluish tinge became their guide. Such was the cow's beauty that the companions couldn't help but stare in admiration, as recounted years later.

Traversing the forest path led by the cow, the group eventually came upon a hut surrounded by wilderness, where an old widow stood at the gate, her eyes clouded by cataracts. Greeted by her unexpectedly sweet voice, she recognized *Bhaba Pagla* as Ram Prashad and invited him to come inside. *Pagla* and his companions, recognizing her as a goddess-like figure, followed her into the house.

As *Bhaba Pagla* and his companions entered the courtyard, they saw a room with a straw roof and a long wooden bench beneath it. On the bench lay a single-stringed musical instrument (ektara), a pair of wooden sandals, but no statues or other artifacts. To the east, there was a bunch of thirty-five sacred trees, perhaps an old memory enshrined by a bamboo fence. *Pagla's* companions realized that this was the sacred dwelling place of Ram Prasad, a holy figure from the past, and they felt honoured to be there.

Tired from their early morning travels and feeling hungry and thirsty, the companions expressed their discomfort to *Pagla*. He told them that there were no shops nearby and suggested they go to the village and bring back some puffed or flattened rice to eat. Hearing his suggestion, they went out towards the village. Meanwhile, *Pagla* and the old lady went to the Panchavati, sitting near the bamboo fence.

Pagla pointed out the spot to the author, indicating that it was a place his previous teacher, *Bhaba Pagla,* had mentioned. About 40 years later, this conversation took place. As *Pagla* and the old lady sat, the old woman offered *Pagla* some rice and coconut. She quickly fetched a coconut with its husk still on, and in a swift motion seemingly cut it into two pieces without any visible instrument, revealing the fresh insides. She then handed the pieces to *Pagla.*

When *Pagla's* companions returned with puffed rice in their clothing, they were hesitant to look at the old lady, whose eyes were clouded by cataracts. As they ate the puffed rice with coconut, they were amazed by the old lady's abilities and the quality of the coconut.

The companions began to explore the area after their meal, leaving two pieces of coconut shell in the muddy platform of the hut. Under the straw roof near the sandals was where *Pagla* and the old lady gathered. She took the coconut shells *Pagla* had set aside and handed them back to him, expressing that she didn't need them returned.

As the group prepared to leave with *Pagla,* they inquired about the old lady's identity. *Pagla,* moved by their curiosity, revealed that she was a form of the Goddess Dhumavati, one of the ten Mahavidyas or great wisdom goddesses. She had appeared out of compassion and then vanished. Baffled and regretful for not having recognized her divine nature, they repented. One of the companions, Bidhu Bhushan, remarked on the importance of the coconut shells she had provided. They decided to keep these shells, marked by the deity's touch, to place in the temple as sacred relics.

The two halves of the coconut shell, still covered with husk, are currently kept in the temple of Maa *Bhaba*ni in Kalna, available for devotees and visitors to see. The minds of Bidhu Bhushan and other companions like Govinda were deeply affected by the address of Ram Prasad, which *Dhumavati,* the Goddess, had used. Twenty-five years since this incident, the dwelling place of Ram Prasad has been renovated and organized for worship, drawing larger public gatherings.

In July 1955, a devotee named Parikshwit Pal was meditating in a corner of the house's courtyard. Deep in contemplation, he offered a silent prayer, pondering whether the cascade of songs from the past had ceased to flow. Parikshwit was from Sodepur-Natagrh, under the district of South 24 Parganas. His father, the late Ashwini Kumar Pal, had been drawn to the songs of Ram Prasad and frequently sang them. This familial connection since childhood likely influenced Parikshwit's own affinity for these spiritual melodies. During his visits to Halisahar, he would engage in meditative recitation of sacred texts.

One day, standing on the banks of the Ganges after his recitations, Parikshwit was awaiting a ferry to Bally when he beheld a saintly vision of *Bhaba Pagla* crossing the sky from Halisahar towards Bally. Though he didn't grasp its meaning, he instinctively saluted the vision with folded hands. A decade later, on August 25, 1967, Parikshwit physically met *Bhaba Pagla*, experiencing a profound sense of joy and reverence that surpassed mere romanticism. He recognized *Pagla* as the same saintly figure he had seen in the sky years prior.

The following evening, Parikshwit saw *Bhaba Pagla* again, this time clearly as Ram Prasad, during a musical gathering. Overwhelmed by a newfound devotional fervour, Parikshwit quickly established a close relationship with *Bhaba Pagla*, marked by blessings and growing intimacy.

On October 16, 1968, a memorable event occurred. Parikshwit approached *Bhaba Pagla*, who was reminiscing about a past event where the Almighty Mother demanded lotus flowers deep at night. *Pagla* recounted to the Mother that he could not find lotus flowers at such an hour. The Mother instructed him to visit a 'Gab' tree, a type of fruit-bearing tree with a thick skin and astringent pulp, assuring him that he would find the lotuses there. Moved by the story, *Bhaba Pagla* asked if the Gab tree was still standing.

On the 23rd of Kartik, Bengali year 1376, corresponding to a date in late autumn, the worship of Goddess Kali, the universal Mother, was about to take place. It was the fourteenth day of the lunar month, which meant that it was the dark night before the new moon. In preparation for the evening's festivities, fourteen lamps were lit at the temple of *Bhaba Pagla* (Babar Shyma Mundir), where the worship of the Almighty Mother would be conducted. *Bhaba Pagla*, having travelled from Kalna, participated in the worship.

That morning, *Pagla* had set a pitcher of water ready for the worship of Goddess Kali at the house of Parikshwit Chandra Pal, a nearby location. After visiting several devotees' homes, *Pagla* arrived and sat in the courtyard of the Baba's temple. There were fifteen more devotees present, along with the owner of the house, Shyama Prasad Saha.

At one point, a song titled "Eber Kali Tomai Khabo" (I shall devote you, Kali) became a topic of conversation. Shyama Prasad Saha inquired, with a hint, whether *Pagla* had composed this song. *Pagla* confirmed that it was indeed composed by Ram Prasad and referred to it as 'Maha Prasad'—a holy offering intended for everyone. *Pagla* expressed the sentiment of the song, dedicating oneself to Goddess Kali and acknowledging her graciousness towards the poor.

Bhaba Pagla then recited the song with haste and a fine tune. His greatly cherished and blessed friend Shanti Ranjan was seated next to him and sang harmoniously while playing the harmonium. The lyrics praised the Mother for satisfying physical hunger and explored various culinary metaphors, culminating in the sentiment of transcending petty desires through spiritual work.

Songs of worship have long been engraved in tradition, first by Ram Prasad and then by other saints such as Kamala Kant. The renowned Ramakrishna and Bama Khayapa did not engage in composing songs themselves, but their worship was significant. This lineage of devotion was continued by *Bhaba Pagla*, whose endless compositions added to the rich tapestry of devotional music.

On that particular morning, when *Pagla* declared himself to be 'Ram Prasad' and 'Maha Prasad', he offered himself as a holy meal—a metaphor for his spiritual offering. This concept struck a chord with Parikshwit Chandra Pal, who was one of *Bhaba Pagla's* most intimate disciples. A profound sense of inspiration took root in Parikshwit's heart, connecting him with the rich tradition of devotional worship and song.

Parikshwit Pal resolved to write an essay titled "Ram Prasad versus Maha Prasad." He harboured a heartfelt wish for *Bhaba Pagla* to write the heading of the essay on a sheet of white paper. Parikshwit decided he would begin his writing only after *Bhaba Pagla* penned the title and signed the paper.

The author, acquainted with Parikshwit like a friend, knew about Parikshwit's request for assistance in having *Bhaba Pagla* write on the paper at every musical function they attended. Eventually, *Bhaba Pagla* visited the Roy residence at Panihati, and Parikshwit seized the opportunity. Parikshwit handed a blank sheet of paper and a pen to the author, imploring him to ask *Pagla* to write 'Ram Prasad' and then 'Maha Prasad' on it.

Following Parikshwit's request, the author presented the paper and pen to *Pagla*, quietly conveying Parikshwit's petition. To their surprise, *Bhaba Pagla* began to inscribe the title onto the paper. The author observed *Pagla's* eyes welling up with tears as he wrote. Upon finishing, *Pagla* confided to the author in a choked voice, revealing the cause of his emotion: it had been many years since he had signed the name 'Ram Prasad,' and this act of reminiscence had moved him deeply. This poignant moment of connection to his spiritual heritage would remain memorable for a lifetime.

****

CHAPTER 11

Episode in Tangile

During a tumultuous episode in Indian history, the political climate was charged due to Gandhi's "Do or Die" movement in 1942. Many misunderstood the movement's intent; there were instances of post offices being burned, looted, and railway tracks being uprooted. The British rulers were on high alert, while Indian servicemen were pressured to suppress their fellow countrymen involved in the movement. Suspicion was rampant, even extending to saints and sages.

Amidst this climate, *Bhaba Pagla* visited the town of Tangile, a place familiar to him since his youth with many followers. His visits to any household in the area would attract crowds keen on listening to his songs. On one occasion, the lawyers and barristers of Tangile invited *Pagla* to the Bar Library Club. Esteemed individuals like Advocate Purnendu Ghosh, Subdivisional Judge Ali Asgar, ICS, and others like Munsif Usha Kanto Babu and Siva Babu warmly welcomed him.

Accompanying *Pagla* were about twelve to fourteen robust young men, including Akhileshwar Lahiri, Ganesh Brahamachari and Nadia Govinda Saha. During that period, young Bengali men often exercised to maintain good health, an activity that the British government regarded with suspicion, deeming it a serious offense.

On the day *Pagla* visited the Bar Library, he brought a violin and bow. As the court session ended, the library filled with people coming to witness *Pagla's* function. Notable figures such as magistrates and civic officials were present. One clever magistrate, attempting to probe *Pagla's* influence, pointed at the young men and asked if they were his disciples and if he was their guru.

In response, *Pagla* sang a song reflecting on the nature of light and darkness, the relationship between the guru and disciple, and the equality of all things in the universe. Through his song, he suggested that the Absolute Brahma is the guru of all, existing without limitations.

During this gathering, Munsi Babu, a smoker, was smoking a cigarette while seated and holding it between two fingers. *Bhaba Pagla,* without commenting on the smoking, started playing his violin. The music captivated Usha Kanta Babu to the extent that he ceased to notice the burning cigarette until it reached his fingertips. It was only later that Munsi Babu realized *Bhaba Pagla's* profound ability in music, almost magical, as he forgot to smoke while enchanted by the tune.

Usha Kanto Babu remarked to others at an event that *Bhaba Pagla* was a world champion with the violin. This sparked some excitement around *Pagla* at the local police station. At the time, the Inspector of Police was Suresh Chakravarthy, who sent two young policemen, Jeevan Krishna Bhattacharya and Chittaranjan Acharya, both around 24 years old, to investigate *Pagla's* activities. With *Bhaba Pagla* attracting large crowds and accompanied by youthful bodybuilders, the police were to follow him discreetly and ascertain his identity.

The Inspector asked Jeevan Krishna and Chittaranjan with finding out who *Pagla* really was. Confident in their police training from Lal Bazaar in Kolkata, they believed they could uncover whatever *Pagla* might be hiding from the British authorities.

The two policemen learned that *Bhaba Pagla* was at the house of Advocate Purnendu Ghosh, the advocate, which was filled to its capacity with visitors. Despite the crowd, they managed to find space to stand in a corner, dressed in plain clothes, pretending to be listeners while they eavesdropped on conversations.

Pagla began to sing a song about the futility of seeking fulfilment in material things and the inner journey of self-discovery. The heartfelt song resonated with the officers, and they found themselves unexpectedly moved.

Bhaba Pagla was known for his attentiveness to attendees at his gatherings, and he would often observe newcomers closely. After the song, he called Jeevan Krishna and Chittaranjan over. They were delighted by the personal invitation and thought they might be able to spot any distinctive marks on *Pagla* to use in their police report.

When Jeevan Krishna approached, *Pagla* inquired with a kind voice what was on his mind. When Jeevan revealed his police service, *Pagla* gently challenged him by asking if he had come to arrest him or to be swayed by his message. Encouraged to sit and listen to the songs, the policemen were disarmed by *Pagla's* warmth and sat down on the floor.

As *Pagla* sang about sadness and love, the disposition of Jeevan and Chittaranjan shifted completely, and they began to question their skeptical stance. Jeevan later expressed a desire to be initiated by *Bhaba Pagla*, who agreed but said the initiation would happen the next day when he would give Jeevan a mantra.

The following day, Jiban Krishna was prepared to receive initiation from *Bhaba Pagla*. He learned that *Pagla* was staying at the house of a coal merchant named Anath Das in Tangile. Eager to honour his soon-to-be guru, Krishna collected Java flowers from a garden near the railway station and fashioned a garland.

Jiban Krishna went to the house of Anath Das with the intention of placing the garland around *Bhaba Pagla's* neck but found that *Pagla* was not there. Leaving the garland and flowers at the house of Anath Das, Krishna searched through different houses until he eventually located *Pagla.*

Returning to Anath's home, Jiban Krishna was startled to see the garland he had made draped around the neck of a statue of Siva a under a Bael (stone apple) tree. It looked splendid, which left Jiban Krishna wondering in surprise if *Pagla* could be Shiva himself.

Jiban Krishna was then initiated by *Bhaba Pagla* under the Bael tree. Three days later, Chittaranjan Acharya also received initiation from *Pagla,* chanting the holy words.

Subsequently, *Bhaba Pagla* visited the home of Manindra Roy at Alisakanta place, accompanied by his two new disciples. Despite their duty obligations, the disciples were compelled by their devotion to follow *Pagla* and were present to witness the warm welcome he received at the Zamindar's house. There, a lavish spread of 80 to 90 different food dishes was prepared for *Pagla.* The music and song function hosted there was extraordinary.

After the event, *Bhaba Pagla* suggested everyone be a little cautious that day, although it seemed to hold no specific importance to anyone aside from him. Later, *Pagla* mentioned his preference to sleep on the cemented bank of a pond, stating that he customarily slept outdoors at night. Many devotees expressed their wish to join him and sleep nearby, desiring to accompany him in this simple practice.

In the custom of our *Pagla,* it was commonplace for people to sleep in the open air at night. On one such occasion, a multitude of devotees—numbering between fifty and sixty—voiced their desire to join the esteemed *Bhaba Pagla* in his nocturnal repose. They assembled on the bank of the pond, forming a large gathering where they all lay down to sleep.

In a gesture of affectionate indulgence, Father *Bhaba Pagla* would rest his head on the lap of each devotee in turn, offering them a moment of delight and personal attention. Ultimately, towards the end of this ritual, he placed his head on the lap of Chittaranjan Acharya. It was around two o'clock at night, and Chittaranjan, who was still awake and filled with contentment, began to tenderly stroke *Bhaba's* hair and body with gentle turns of his fingers.

Bhaba Pagla, inquiring suddenly, asked Chittaranjan to "run jump" despite the late hour. Upon learning that it was indeed 2 AM, Chittaranjan, who had sat awake the entire night, neither sleeping nor moving from his spot continued to softly chant holy words and devotedly tend to *Bhaba Pagla.*

Bhaba Pagla, meanwhile, laid his head upon a wooden seat and covered himself with a blue quilt and a wrapper, while Chittaranjan remained seated beside him, ever vigilant. The mantra and holy name resonated with greater intensity in Chittaranjan's mind as he immersed himself in his spiritual practice.

The night was quiet, darkened by the phase of the moon just after the new moon, and the pond's water shimmered in the faint moonlight. Above the serene setting stretched a vast blue sky, creating a picturesque nocturnal scene. Then, unexpectedly, a ball of light that paralleled the moon's luminance appeared on the right-side bank of the pond. Chittaranjan watched in wonder as this orb of light approached a dense mango tree on the eastern bank and then suddenly disappeared.

In the following moments, Chittaranjan experienced a startling sensation as he felt *Bhaba Pagla's* limbs grow rigid. The bewilderment was short-lived, however, for as he turned his gaze, he beheld a divine presence; a beautiful girl clothed in a brown sari.

On the bank of the pond, Chittaranjan noticed his revered guru, *Bhaba Pagla,* standing beside a beautiful girl who appeared as if she could be from a wealthy landlord's family. It seemed as though she had come in secret to convey a message to *Bhaba Pagla.* But there was something unique about today; Chittaranjan could see that *Bhaba Pagla* was engaged in a divine interaction, holding a special oblong water pot meticulously crafted. Together, the girl and *Bhaba Pagla* walked along the cemented bank of the pond, circumambulating the sleeping devotees. After around five minutes, the woman disappeared.

Time passed until, by Chittaranjan's side, *Bhaba Pagla,* who had been sleeping, suddenly chanted "Kali Kali", and his body relaxed back to normality. Chittaranjan, bewildered by what he had witnessed, confided in *Bhaba Pagla* who informed him that he was fortunate to have seen the Almighty Mother.

As dawn approached and morning settled in, Central Jin, near the Shiva temple of the house, was approached by Jeevan Krishna. Suddenly, Chittaranjan announced that the Almighty Mother was imminent, as he could see footprints and was overwhelmed by a pleasant smell. He questioned Jeevan Krishna if he could also perceive it. After wiping the temple floor with a handkerchief and taking a whiff, Chittaranjan confirmed the indescribably sweet and pleasant odour. When offered to Jeevan Krishna, he too sensed the delightful fragrance and bowed to honour Chittaranjan with abundant devotion. Although Chittaranjan was reluctant to allow it, Jeevan Krishna insisted on touching his feet in reverence. In a tender moment, they touched heads in a mutual sign of respect.

In this memorable incident that unfolded in the life of Jeevan Krishna, the Police Inspector of the Tangile Subdivision, he was at his office absorbed in the meditation and recitation of his Guru's mantra. Meanwhile, *Bhaba Pagla* was at the Amta house temple with some devotees and disciples when he cryptically announced that Jeevan was calling for him and requested no one to touch his body before lying down and covering himself with a blue cloth wrapper.

The attendees alternately regarded the venerated temple deity and *Bhaba Pagla,* covered under the blue wrapper, and recognized Jeevan Krishna Bhattacharya's strong connection. To their astonishment, they noticed under the cloth that *Bhaba Pagla's* form was thinning gradually.

Concurrently, during his meditation at the police post, Jeevan Krishna vividly envisioned *Bhaba Pagla* in the courtyard. His wonder was palpable as he saw *Bhaba Pagla* appear in a tangible form. Filled with joy, Jeevan Krishna leapt from his chair and hastened towards the courtyard where he had seen the vision, but upon approaching, *Bhaba Pagla* simply smiled and then vanished. Jeevan Krishna proceeded to the same courtyard, and over it, there was a bamboo fence, yet the presence of *Bhaba Pagla* lingered in the air.

Chittaranjan Acharya, the devoted son of *Bhaba Pagla,* was warmly welcomed into the home of the person he affectionately referred to as his father. The encounter took place on December 31, 1970. Their conversation touched on various topics, including Chittaranjan's spiritual experiences and his professional life.

Chittaranjan's host expressed an eagerness to learn about the events that led to Chittaranjan's resignation from the police service and asked him to share the details of his life from that point forward. Chittaranjan responded by expressing his profound reverence for *Bhaba Pagla,* declaring his understanding of him as both Shiva and the Almighty Mother incarnate. He remarked on the divine traits of *Bhaba Pagla,* who would float in the sky and yet, he was remarkably accessible to even the humblest of his followers, preferring to be called by his name rather than an honourific title such as 'Gurudeva.'

Chittaranjan went on to recount an incident from his time in the police service. Once, during his stint at a police station, he was drawn to a celebration of songs and music dedicated to *Bhaba Pagla.* Unable to resist the pull, he left his duty post to join the festivities, missing his assignment the following day. The station had been visited by a European Superintendent Sahab, and Chittaranjan feared repercussions including potential dismissal from his job. However, upon his return to the station, he discovered that no report had been filed against him; another individual had been mistaken for him and marked as on duty—a turn of events he attributed to the grace of *Bhaba Pagla.*

He then spoke of another time when he received orders from his superiors to confront a group of dacoits 20 miles away. The route involved navigating a channel and a deep tank by boat, a daunting task given the dangers posed by the dacoits. Yet, invoking the name of his Guru, he managed the mission successfully with divine support. In another instance, he was charged by high officials to permanently quell the threat of dacoits in the subdivision of Kishoregunj, where the disturbances were rampant. Accepting the challenge, he and his armed team sailed on the Brahmaputra River and encountered a large number of dacoits. Chittaranjan disembarked from the boat and anchored it at a little distance, then swam in the river to close the distance stealthily, while his boat followed. His narrative showcased not only his deep spirituality but also his courage and sense of duty.

Chittaranjan Acharya daringly submerged himself into the river to stealthily approach the boat of dacoits. Amidst the storm with thunder roaring and lightning flashing, he heard a voice resounding in his ears, "Don't be afraid." Bolstered by the encouragement, he continued his advance. When he neared the dacoits, they spotted him and lunged to attack him with large, curved blades. Miraculously, he sustained no injuries despite being struck twice; had he been wounded, he may not have escaped.

During the confrontation, eight to ten dacoits were wounded by the police gunfire, some fatally, and the entire gang was successfully subdued. For this feat, Chittaranjan was later awarded the Viceroy's Medal.

On another occasion, Chittaranjan had duties in a village known for its hazardous crematorium, a place steeped in superstition. Accompanied by Jeevan Babu, they ventured together into the crematorium. There, amid the silence, they perceived a divine light and had a clear vision of the goddess Kali, the Adi Shakti, and heard the jingling of her anklets, an experience they attributed to the grace of their Guru.

When asked about his home, Chittaranjan revealed he was from the district of Barishal, near the Jhalkati railway station. His post-government domestic life was challenging; his departure from service had caused dissatisfaction among his peers. Yet he devoted his days to worship, meditation, and the recitation of holy words. With the country's partition, his family could no longer reside in Barishal and relocated to West Bengal, settling in the Satin Sen colony of New Barrackpore, in a community that started as slums.

Chittaranjan recounted another incident where he acted with compelling bravery. A factory producing medicine near the slums caught fire due to a petroleum spill. Instantly invoking *Bhaba Pagla,* Chittaranjan entered the blazing room and miraculously extinguished the fire without any harm befalling himself.

He also spoke of a sublime experience in May 1972, when a new Kali temple was established in New Barrackpore. Chittaranjan was entrusted with the temple's worship rituals. One midnight, during his service, he underwent a mystical transformation but couldn't comprehend the change. Suddenly he heard *Bhaba Pagla's* voice whispering, "Kali, come in. Kali, come in," it echoed through the night. Then, at three in the morning, he distinctly heard chanting, after which he beheld a wondrous vision of the Almighty Mother standing before him for an extended period, as though *Bhaba Pagla* had himself become a child aged six. Struggling to grasp the significance of this vision, Chittaranjan felt deeply connected to his old master.

Chittaranjan Acharya passionately implored Master, the author of book "Param Guru Bhaba Pagla" to listen attentively to his experiences following his resignation from the police service. He explained that after leaving his job, he was unable to directly seek blessings from *Bhaba Pagla,* as he had returned to his hometown of Bishnupur. Subsequently, the country underwent partition, and *Bhaba Pagla* moved across the new border, making it difficult for Chittaranjan to maintain visual contact with his guru.

Despite this, Chittaranjan remained eager to learn of *Bhaba Pagla's* whereabouts, prompting the author to reassure him that he maintained connections with those who were in touch with the saintly figure. The author promised to inform Chittaranjan if there was an opportunity to meet *Bhaba Pagla,* assuring him of a future reunion.

Chittaranjan reminisced about *Bhaba Pagla's* letters, noting how the saint would write "let me see your appearance" rather than requesting a visit. This endearing phrase emphasized *Bhaba Pagla's* unique and incomparable nature, as well as the depth of his affection for his devotees.

Bhaba Pagla visited the home of Gopal Bandyopadhyay, the controller of Calcutta University, at Belghoria was during the month of Magh as per Bengali calendar, corresponding to mid-January to mid-February, the same year. A function of songs and music was held at Gopal Basu's residence, drawing a substantial crowd that afternoon, which included distinguished individuals such as a judge of the Calcutta High Court, the principal of Bengal Music College, and others who were present at that time.

Chittaranjan Acharya, along with a group of 10 to 12 people, arrived at the entrance of the event. He had been about 30 or 31 years old when he left the police service, and presently he was nearing the age of 60. Upon seeing Chittaranjan at the doorway, *Bhaba Pagla* greeted him warmly, calling out "Are you,

Chittaranjan? Come here, come here." This heartfelt welcome signified a profound moment of affection and devotion. Chittaranjan was deeply moved and puzzled by the incomparable presence of *Bhaba Pagla*, questioning what parallel could ever be drawn to such a remarkable and spiritual individual.

****

CHAPTER 12

Welcome Invitation by Nawab of Murshidabad

In 1946, the Nawab of Murshidabad had heard many accounts of *Bhaba Pagla,* who was renowned for his philanthropy, his equal sympathy towards all castes and religions, and his simple, unorthodox lifestyle. Additionally celebrated for his talents in singing and music, the Nawab's curiosity to meet *Bhaba Pagla* was piqued.

To fulfill this desire, the Nawab arranged for an invitation to be sent to *Bhaba Pagla* to visit Navab Bhavan in Murshidabad. The Nawab dispatched a letter along with some money to extend this invitation. However, *Bhaba Pagla,* upon receiving the letter, responded with laughter and remarked that 'sending a letter would get a letter' and 'a man is to be sent to bring a man.' Instead of following the request, *Bhaba Pagla* used the money to feed people, thus the Nawab's initial attempt to meet him was unsuccessful. Nevertheless, the Nawab realized his mistake and took a different approach when he learned that *Bhaba Pagla* had made his way to Kolkata. He enlisted Amalendu Bagchi, who owned a new motor car, to personally fetch *Bhaba Pagla.*

When Bagchi reached *Bhaba Pagla* with the car, he encountered an unexpected problem; the car would not start, despite the driver's best efforts. Eventually, a companion of *Bhaba Pagla* suggested that the car would not move without the holy man's consent. Upon Bagchi's respectful request, *Bhaba Pagla* permitted them to begin the journey and jovially told the driver to start the car, which then started smoothly.

Years later, in 1970, *Bhaba Pagla* visited the Roy Bati house at Panihati in the district of North 24 Parganas. During his stay, songs composed by *Bhaba Pagla* were sung throughout the day-long event. That evening, the function attracted a significant gathering, including a cloth merchant from Bowbazar who arrived with a group in his car. After enjoying the music and *Bhaba Pagla's* powerful words upstairs, the group descended to leave for Kolkata without seeking *Bhaba Pagla's* permission to depart, a courtesy typically observed.

Observing their leave-taking, *Bhaba Pagla*, seated nearby, jokingly asked if he should halt their vehicle. At his implied consent, *Bhaba Pagla* symbolically made a fist and, as if wielding mystical influence, extended his arm. True to his gesture, the merchant's car refused to start despite multiple efforts over 15 minutes. It was then suggested to the merchant to request *Bhaba Pagla's* permission to leave, as the car would not move otherwise. Upon realizing the oversight, the merchant went back upstairs, confessed the car's troubles to *Bhaba Pagla*, and sought his permission to leave. With a benevolent "Come again, my son," from *Bhaba Pagla*, the car started without further issue.

Similarly, on another day, the author observed a group of sages who drove to meet *Bhaba Pagla* from their hermitage. They spent joyful time with the revered saint, listening to many of his compositions. However, like the merchant, they too left without asking for leave. As a result, they encountered mechanical issues and had to return to ask *Bhaba Pagla's* permission before their car would function again, teaching everyone the value of a simple courtesy in the presence of someone so esteemed.

The strange behaviour witnessed was not a mere childlike whimsy from *Bhaba Pagla*; rather, it served as either a playful display of his magical or miraculous abilities or as a lesson meant for those present. However, digressing momentarily from the tale at hand, we return to Amalendu Bagchi's effort in escorting *Bhaba Pagla* to Murshidabad.

Upon arrival in Murshidabad, *Bhaba Pagla* initially stayed at the residence of Mr. Bagchi. It wasn't long before *Bhaba Pagla* proceeded to meet the Nawab who had been longing to see him. As people thronged to catch a glimpse of *Bhaba Pagla,* he greeted the Nawab with an endearing reference, calling him 'my son,' and asked how the Nawab came to know him. With gentle reproach, *Bhaba Pagla* said, "We come from the same Malik (God); we are brothers. Shall I not be able to know you?" Those present witnessed firsthand the profound connection *Bhaba Pagla* shared with others through just a few words. *Bhaba Pagla* was deeply loved because he extended his love to everyone, making them feel as though they were his own.

During this journey, *Bhaba Pagla* remained in the city for four and a half months—a lapse originally intended to last only four days. Wherever *Bhaba Pagla* was, there was music, sweet conversation, and numerous memorable incidents that naturally attracted people to gather around.

In the earlier part of the month at Keshab Chakraborty's residence, an incident occurred involving an inspector of police named Shambhu Nath Paul. He expressed doubt about *Bhaba Pagla's* authenticity in a crowd, prompting *Bhaba Pagla*—who was always sharply attentive—to challenge the inspector with, "What did you say, my son?" Upon realizing his mistake, Shambhu Nath quickly understood the caution in his words and soon, along with his family, became a devout follower of *Bhaba Pagla.* When he was later transferred to the Shantipur police station, he invited *Bhaba Pagla* several times to his home. His daughter, Madhuri, learned many songs from *Bhaba Pagla* and would accompany him in singing these compositions across different regions.

Throughout *Bhaba Pagla's* duration in Murshidabad, he was regularly adorned with garlands of beautiful flowers presented by the gardener Lakshmi Narayan, acting on the Nawab's instructions. One particular night, at 10 o'clock in the home of the Bagchis, a different vision of restlessness in *Bhaba Pagla* captivated Bagchi, as *Bhaba Pagla* exhibited signs of spiritual fervour and disturbance.

Bhaba Pagla exhibited intense restlessness, pacing back and forth and only uttering the words "stop, stab" repeatedly. The very next day, news broke out that riots had erupted in Kolkata. Violence spread to multiple locations, with casualties and the sources of the incendiary words remaining unaccounted for.

After spending four and a half months in Murshidabad, it was time for *Bhaba Pagla* to return home. On his departure, Lakshmi, the gardener, garlanded *Bhaba Pagla* around his neck for the last time. This prompted someone to inquire whether Lakshmi had been giving something to *Bhaba Pagla* every day with the garlands. His immediate response was quizzical, and *Bhaba Pagla* himself retorted to the query by asking why, with all their collective eyes, they hadn't observed what he had given to Lakshmi. The question left everyone speechless, and *Bhaba Pagla* elaborated that each time he received a garland, he would extend his neck to wear it and internally recited the name of the Almighty Mother with each instance. This disclosure once again silenced the listeners.

Bhaba Pagla was known to use humour to lift the spirits of his devotees, preferring they not dwell in sadness or solemn introspection. It was perhaps out of a desire to shift the mood during his departure that he posed a mystical riddle to the crowd: "We all remain in the same room, we possess fire in our heart, coming heads coming out from the womb, the striated body of the mother. We are destroyed by burning to ashes because of that same. Tell me what it is." Met with a moment of collective silence, none of the attendees could fathom an answer, until *Bhaba Pagla* himself provided the solution by referring to a matchbox and its sticks.

With this parting insight, the people present were given a glimpse of *Bhaba Pagla's* unique perspective—a teaching moment that was emblematic of the rarity of such saints in India.

****

CHAPTER 13

A Great Poet of Unification

In the wake of the tumultuous violence and unrest that erupted in 1946—a period marked by a struggle for India's independence and the painful partition that followed—peace remained elusive. With the creation of East Pakistan, now known as Bangladesh, tensions continued to simmer. Amidst this backdrop, a significant incident unfolded in the village of Garparah in East Bengal.

Khurshed Alam was a respected figure in the area, known for his role as a Hakeem (a traditional medicine practitioner) and his reputation as a just judge who transcended communal biases. His physical stature was substantial, yet it was his impartiality that truly made him stand out. Alam took prompt action upon receiving troubling news from Garparah: a potential conflict loomed over a shared space where Hindus had organized a Kali Puja worship event on an open field, and right in front of them, Muslims planned to conduct a Korbani, a religious festival.

The proximity of these religious functions brewed mutual suspicion and escalating debates between the groups, fostering an environment ripe for conflict. Alam, well-informed about the historical tensions, including the devastating riots of Noakhali in 1946 which had deeply affected Mahatma Gandhi, was determined to prevent another communal clash.

At the heart of this brewing confrontation stood the venerated *Bhaba Pagla*, a figure revered by both Hindus and Muslims alike for his teachings and spiritual guidance. It was known that *Bhaba*

Pagla had visited the house of Mohini Ghosh in Garparah, which fortified Alam's resolve to seek his intervention.

Recognizing the gravity of the situation, Alam proposed a solution to the village's predicaments to both parties. He suggested, with his acute wisdom, "If doubts and disagreements persist among you, let *Bhaba Pagla* resolve them. Why exhaust ourselves with these problems when he can provide judgment? What do you say? Isn't that a good plan? If you agree, I will bring *Bhaba Pagla* to address your issues." As expected, the suggestion was warmly accepted, as *Bhaba Pagla's* appeal and wisdom were unanimously acknowledged by both communities, who had deep regard for him.

Thus, on the request of Khurshed Alam, *Bhaba Pagla* made his appearance in Garparah. His presence immediately commanded reverence from everyone gathered. Both Hindus and Muslims, united in their respect for the saintly figure, bowed their heads at the feet of *Bhaba Pagla* as a gesture of homage.

Through his divine influence and profound understanding of humanity, *Bhaba Pagla* successfully navigated the tense situation and fostered an atmosphere of unity. His approach effectively dissolved the hatred, suspicions, and potential for conflict, demonstrating his unique ability to transcend communal divides and bring peace to the troubled region.

Khurshed Alam conveyed the tense situation to *Bhaba Pagla,* though his elaboration was scarcely needed as the saint was already aware of the unfolding events. *Pagla* addressed Khurshed directly, declaring that the gathered assembly had already reached their own judgment, leaving them astonished and eager to hear more from him, well aware that his words often carried deeper, insightful meanings.

Bhaba Pagla highlighted the apparent differences between the groups, noting how the Muslim organizers, mainly from the peasant class, sat directly on the earthen ground, whereas the Hindu participants, who were predominantly middle-class 'Babus', had seated themselves on mats spread on the ground. He poignantly asked each group where they were seated, and upon hearing their responses, he posed a question to everyone: "Did you listen to their answers? One group says they have sat on 'Madur,' (a kind of mat), while these people are saying they sat on the 'Mati' ground, the earthen soil. By the word Madur *Pagla* meant – distant from Mother and the word Mati meant on the lap of Ma (Mother), in Bengali. So, who among you is closer to the Almighty Mother Ma?" This pun was met with laughter, dispelling the tension that had weighed upon the village.

When a young Muslim expressed that they do not revere the goddess Kali, *Bhaba Pagla* challenged this viewpoint with humour and wisdom. He spoke of how, despite religious differences, the name 'Kali' is woven into the fabric of their lives, not just as a deity but as a measurement of cultivated land and crop yields. *Pagla* argued that by using the term in everyday life, they inadvertently paid respect to the goddess, sparking waves of laughter among the crowd.

Pagla skillfully disarmed the debate by revealing the shared linguistic and cultural threads that connected everyone, regardless of faith. He implored the youth to look beyond superficial divisions, reminding them that the very earth and straw they toiled over were used to construct the goddess Kali's idols. His words implored them to recognize the sanctity in their labour and the materials they worked with, fostering a sense of respect and realization.

Bhaba Pagla continued, urging them to think deeper and perceive the interconnectedness of all things. In his discourse, he invoked the profound spiritual concept that everything, including the universe, the sky, the earth, and the ether, is infused with the essence of Kali—encompassing both the divine and the mundane.

Through his songs and teachings, *Pagla* infused the gathering with a sense of wonder and contemplation, using his presence and intellect to bridge the divide and guide both communities toward greater understanding and harmony.

Bhaba Pagla spoke to the gathered people, sharing wisdom that touched upon the principles of mathematics as a metaphor for life's journey. "If you strip away worldly desires, you won't struggle to learn the art of subtraction," he advised. He suggested that by counting affectionately, one could naturally learn to subtract, and as a result, the multiplication of joy would flourish. The pleasure of division, he explained, is found in the law of love. He pointed out that fortune does not favour the unfortunate, and those who are consumed by folly solve equations only for the sake of solving them, missing the underlying essence of being nestled in the Almighty Mother's lap.

Bhaba Pagla drew an analogy between the act of holding a mathematical problem ('Onko' in Bengali) in the mind and cradling a child on a mother's lap, indicating a sense of closeness and care. He spoke of composing arithmetic as if it were an act of devotion, fully surrendering oneself to the spiritual process.

Through his teaching, *Bhaba Pagla* inspired delight among his devotees, helping them forget their differences and come together in a state of collective joy. He emphasized that he did not wish to punish but rather aimed to cultivate peace among the people, making him a pivotal figure in uniting them. Truly, *Bhaba Pagla* was not just a spiritual teacher of individual paths but also a unifier of collective thought.

As the audience hung onto his every word, *Bhaba Pagla* shared insights on yoga, a union of spiritual thoughts, and pointed out that true worship did not rely on the physical representation of gods or the sacrifice of animals. Instead, he maintained that the true sacrifice was to let go of animalistic thoughts and behaviours, and if one realized the presence of the Almighty Mother, there would be no need for constructing statues or performing ritual sacrifices.

He criticized the tendency to chant mantras without understanding or to build statues for worship without genuine connection. *Pagla* sang about the folly in such practices, questioning the need for material representations when the goal was to internalize the divine presence. He encouraged the people to consider that every technique and magic they sought was already part of the wonder of the Almighty Mother's world.

Bhaba Pagla used song as a tool to awaken and surprise the people, leading them to question their understanding of spirituality. He humbly admitted that he did not claim to know everything; instead, he attributed his insight to the divine magic of the Almighty Mother. His listeners were left pondering their existence and the confusions they faced in life.

In conclusion, *Bhaba Pagla* urged his devotees to remember that those who err are haunted by the ghosts of their problems. By recognizing and learning from their mistakes, they would find the truth. He questioned whether they wished to perpetuate the memory of violence in society or rather contribute to a legacy of universal love and unity among all people.

Bhaba Pagla spoke to the gathered crowd, urging unity and affection. "Do you not wish to say that we belong to the same brethren? That we should remain side by side, bound by affection?" he implored. He called on everyone to nurture a femininity of beautiful mind—a metaphor perhaps for gentleness and empathy. He invited his listeners to reflect on a song with a poignant message: Remember, no one is permanent in this world; don't prioritize your interests alone, but regard everyone as your own kin.

"Oh mind," *Bhaba Pagla* sang, "you are engrossed in your own interests, blind to the hearts of others. Why do you try to hide your faults by pointing out the mistakes of others? If you keep your mind open, you will find no pain or problems will come your way. You will experience the joy of love daily, becoming part of the carnival of affection. Remain humane, for the God above, a figure of wonder, will guide us all. Consider the true value of life and learn from the words of Baba."

Moved by his song, the people embraced each other tightly, as if they were reuniting with long-lost family. They gazed towards the heavens, calling out loudly the name of *Bhaba Pagla,* affirming the saint's role as a unifying force and a great man. Together, with reverence and respect, they saluted him by saying in unison, "Sir, Salam, Pranam," an acknowledgment of the deep impact *Bhaba Pagla* had on fostering a sense of unity and brotherhood among them.

****

CHAPTER 14

The Rising in the East and Setting in the West

As time marches on, the multifaceted events of history unfold within its boundless tapestry. The anecdotes of history, tinged with both joy and sorrow, are shaped by the dichotomy of good and evil within human society, as moments of happiness and grief leave their impressions upon the world. Throughout the ages, the annals of history have chronicled events influenced by both the virtuous and the ignoble behaviours of humankind.

India, in particular, has borne witness to violent upheavals due to the malicious actions of foreign invaders and internal terrorists. The peace, cultural richness, and progress of Indian civilization have, at times, been jeopardized by these malevolent forces. Names like Sultan Mahmud, Taimur Lang, Nadir Shah, Genghis Khan, Jalaluddin Mohammad Shah, Alauddin Khilji, and others dot the landscape of India's past with accounts of strife and conflict. With the advent of colonial powers such as Britain, France, and Portugal, a new chapter of violence unfolded, marked by bloodshed and the anguish of innocent lives.

A division arose within India, fuelled by a faction of selfish individuals who sought to cleave the nation based on religious lines. These separatists, native to the very soil they aimed to split, threatened ongoing civil war unless India was partitioned. In doing so, they exhibited a tragic lapse in wisdom and foresight, as the loss of reason often paves the way to destruction. Stubbornly committed to the division of India, they failed to appreciate the value of harmonious coexistence.

Echoing this divisive sentiment, the British colonial government supported the partition of India at the end of their rule. Their position was that India should be divided according to the two-nation theory, paving the way for prolonged enmity and hostility between the newly formed nations of India and Pakistan. This strategy ensured the dissipating influence of Britain would leave behind a legacy of conflict.

The consequences were dire: the land that was once holy, where people lived as brethren, was now stained with the blood of its children. The meagre possessions of the poor, accumulated through arduous labour, were laid to waste in the fires of violence. The subcontinent was severed in two by the policy of the British government, and even the lush, prosperous Bengal was split asunder.

Those from East Bengal, once integral to the cultural, educational, and service fabric of India and who had held positions of respect, now found themselves foreigners on their native land. The Partition created an abyss between fellow Bengalis, as people were forced to abandon their ancestral homes, the sacred remembrance of their cremation grounds, and the hallowed temples where generations had kindled oil lamps and revered the holy Tulsi plant.

Families that once reunited joyously during the Durga Puja festival were now silenced by the cunning manoeuvres of politicians. The peaceful tenor of the nation was shattered, leading to ongoing violence, particularly against the Hindu minority population in Muslim-majority areas. The persecution persisted, largely due to the two-nation theory which had sown seeds of division.

Amidst this turmoil, the revered poet of unity, *Bhaba Pagla*, stood as a beacon in East Bengal. Despite the chaos, the worship of the Maa Manasa continued in the ancestral home of Dakshin Ray, a testament to the resilience of faith and tradition in the face of sweeping change.

In a climate of escalating tensions, not all heeded the virtue-laden messages of great leaders. Despite this, there remained a steadfast group of disciples and devotees, Hindu and Muslim alike, who followed the teachings of *Bhaba Pagla*. However, conflict arose when a group of zealous young members of the Muslim party confronted *Bhaba Pagla* and began to denounce the Shaligram Shila, a holy stone revered by Hindus, an act which *Pagla* could not ignore.

The cruelty inflicted upon Hindus grew intolerable, and they began to flee East Pakistan (formerly East Bengal) in large numbers. Witnessing such abhorrent acts toward the Hindus weighed heavily on *Bhaba Pagla*, reminding him of the pain he bore years earlier when violence and killings erupted in Kolkata. He recalled a time when he resided in the home of the king, Amalendu Bagchi, in Murshidabad and became consumed by restlessness and repetitive utterances of "Stop, Stop, Stop," as if attempting to halt the violence through his words.

Amid this reflection, *Pagla* wondered whether the people of Kolkata had forgotten him, only to reassure himself that they had not. Ganga Charan Saha and his brother-in-law, Vinod Bihari Roy, contemplated the duration of *Pagla's* continued presence amidst such suffering in East Bengal. Ganga Charan requested his brother-in-law to compose a letter, not just any letter, but one that would resonate with *Bhaba Pagla* and urge him to come to Kolkata. This letter eventually reached *Pagla*, sparking a cascade of profound contemplation within him, as if a new chapter was dawning in his heart and mind.

As the landscape of East Bengal changed following Partition, *Bhaba Pagla's* childhood friends and many other acquaintances had migrated to West Bengal. Among them, some settled in Kolkata while others found homes beyond.

During these tumultuous times, Tejen Mondal, a devout follower of *Bhaba Pagla*, visited him at Amta. Originally from Manikganj, Tejen's professional life revolved around large batches of machinery. Concurrently, Hem Banerjee, a wealthy heir accustomed to luxurious living since childhood, was profoundly impacted by his association with *Bhaba Pagla.* Overwhelmed by love for the saint, Hem found himself drawn away from opulence, with no qualms about embracing a more ordinary existence.

Seeking guidance, he appealed to *Bhaba Pagla*, lamenting his indolence and inability to awaken early in the morning. With compassion, *Pagla* penned a poetic song as an offering to Hem, instructing him to rise at dawn and chant the name of Kali, the goddess. The song detailed a ritual of purification involving the plucking of Jaba flowers and leaves from the stone apple (Bael) tree to create an offering. It encouraged devotional worship, stating that the indolence of the mind would be dispelled by such acts of reverence, calling out "Shiva, Shiva," so that one might seek shelter at the feet of the Almighty Mother and remove ignorance through joyful celebration.

Bhaba Pagla told Hem Banerjee to sing a song he had composed, assuring him that it would help dispel his laziness. Once Hem learned the tune of the song, he found himself transformed and made his way to Amta, where *Pagla* resided.

In the year 1357 of the Bengali calendar, which corresponds to 1950 in the Engilish calendar, during the month of Baishakh, *Bhaba Pagla* decided to move his family to West Bengal. He sent his wife Saibalini, and his daughter, Pratima (six- to seven-year-old), his eldest son Sanat Kumar (twelve) and his youngest son of

Sankalpa (three) along with Tejen Mondal and Hem Banerjee for relocation.

The family found refuge in the town of Jiaganj in Murshidabad, taking shelter with the disciple Vijay Krishna, a devout follower of *Bhaba Pagla.* Another disciple, Bimal Kundu, whose house was in Lal Baug, Shahanagar, not far from Kutubpur, would take responsibility for the family as instructed by *Bhaba Pagla.* Bimal ensured that *Pagla's* wife and children could reside safely at Kutubpur. Tejen Mondal would frequently travel between Murshidabad, Amta, and Dhaka, relaying news and transporting household items as needed.

Amidst all this activity, there was much speculation among the people as to whether *Pagla* would leave Amta for Kolkata or not. He himself remained silent, calm as the Pacific Ocean, yet equally restless to act when necessary. People sometimes thought of him as mad, but *Bhaba Pagla* was a 'thoughtful madman,' deeply intentional in his seeming unpredictability.

"When you all come to visit me, you may wonder who's truly mad—me, the '*Pagla,*' or perhaps you," he would playfully say, igniting murmurs around the village about his potential departure. Mahini Mohan Ghosh's family from Garparah, near Amta, along with others from the region, were prepared to follow *Bhaba Pagla* if he decided to move to Kolkata.

Leaving Amta, however, was not an easy decision for *Bhaba Pagla,* given the many surrounding villages like Baliya, Baliyati, Garparah, Kedarpur, Dighlia, Nagpur, Tangile, Chowhat river, to name a few, that housed thousands of disciples who had participated in and witnessed countless events in *Bhaba Pagla's* life.

In Amta, a significant sum of 26,000 rupees was spent hosting a grand worship of the goddess Anandamayi. At that time, a maund of rice, weighing about 40 seers (approximately 37.5 kilograms), cost two rupees. During these large-scale worship events, accompanied by songs and music, festive fairs would take place annually. Large bamboo baskets were used to distribute muri (puffed rice) mixed with chanachur (chickpeas) to every home in the area. *Bhaba Pagla* himself would hand out these snacks from the baskets, inviting people to eat and enjoy the puffed rice mixture whenever they came to pay respects. For *Bhaba Pagla*, everything about these occasions was wonderful.

Sensing a shift in the atmosphere, *Bhaba Pagla* suddenly expressed that he felt hungry and wanted to have curd. This recollection was shared with us by a palanquin bearer from Amta to Saturi. As if by providence, a bullock cart arrived at that moment, laden with earthen containers filled with curd. All present there, partook of the curd, their hunger satiated, and *Bhaba Pagla* often attributed such serendipitous events to the grace of the Almighty Mother. Leaving behind a place replete with captivating and memorable incidents was no simple decision, but *Bhaba Pagla* was not one to be bound by the illusions of the world.

The departure from Amta was prompted by communication from the family of Mohini Ghosh from Garparah. Finally, *Bhaba Pagla* set out for Kolkata in West Bengal. The date of departure was the fourth day of Jaistha, a Friday, in the year 1357 of the Bengali calendar (the year 1950 as per the English calendar). Among those who accompanied him were Ganesh Brahamchari, Karthik Chakravarty, Hem Banerjee, his nephew Amar Govinda Saha, Tejen Mondal, Lalu Takhur (Nirmaleshwar Lahiri), Mohini Ghosh with his wife, his daughter Nilima, their son Malaya, and others.

Upon reaching the dock for the steamer boat, a Muslim Sub-Inspector of Police named Reza Sahab, alongside a group of policemen, stood before *Bhaba Pagla*. Rather than speaking with a tone of threat, the inspector expressed his feelings in a pleading manner, asking why *Pagla* was leaving and questioning whether they had shown him less love. When *Bhaba Pagla* mentioned the force he possessed, he was speaking not of physical strength, but of a spiritual force signified by clasped hands—the universal symbol of prayer and unity.

The situation became emotional, with the devoted inspector Reza Sahab's tearful eyes. Wanting to shift the mood, *Bhaba Pagla* turned to light-hearted humour. He played on the Bengali word for "gun," which also means "sing," jesting that while bullets might run out, the songs ('gun' as in singing) are never-ending.

Pagla then humorously pledged to the inspector that just as the sun rises in the east and sets in the west, he had spent the first half of his life in East Bengal, and now, as evening approached, he would continue his journey in West Bengal. It was the rainy season when *Bhaba Pagla* boarded a boat at Amta, headed for Garaparah. From there, he travelled to Goaland Ghat, boarding a train at Darshana station on the border, a route plagued by plunderers who troubled evacuees from East Bengal by ransacking their valuables.

Pagla, along with his 15 to 16 companions carrying valuable items and possessions, vigilantly transported a black stone statue of Ma Anandamayi, the Almighty Mother, carefully enclosed within a wooden box.

The wooden box, meticulously packed, drew the attention of the plunderers, who mistakenly believed it contained valuable materials. Upon reaching out to open the box, Nilima, a dear disciple of *Bhaba Pagla,* could no longer restrain her anguish. Overcome with emotion, she exclaimed to *Bhaba Pagla,* questioning why he remained silent amid the unfolding events.

Bhaba Pagla replied to Nilima in a tranquil tone, advising her that it was better not to alert the other travellers in the same compartment to the plunderers' activities, as they focused on unscrewing and unveiling the contents of the box. However, as the plunderers forcefully pried open the box and struck the statue within, *Bhaba Pagla* felt a corresponding pain in his back. In what seemed a spiritual connection to the statue, two carbuncles emerged on his back, one on each side, and their healing was prolonged.

For the first time, *Pagla* allowed a doctor to administer an injection to alleviate the condition. When questioned about taking medicine, someone remarked that poison destroys poison. *Bhaba Pagla's* response, characteristically enigmatic, was to embrace the "poison" with resignation, saying, "Well, my son, let this poison remain in my body."

Bhaba Pagla's presence in Kolkata was not new; he had frequented the city since his youth. However, this time his arrival heralded a different purpose. His odyssey as a resident of East Bengal had concluded, and now he began a fresh chapter in West Bengal. The closure of his earlier life brought about the commencement of a miraculous new phase. *Bhaba Pagla's* ambition was to cultivate a garden of spirituality, fostering unity between the East Bengalis of what was now Pakistan and the people of West Bengal, India.

The extraordinary events that transpired in West Bengal would soon be relayed in the second part of this book, marking *Pagla's* story as a singular phenomenon in India's spiritual history.

****

Author's Note

This Author's Note emphasizes the value of spiritual growth, self-discovery, and balance in the face of societal expectations, highlighting the accessibility of spiritual enlightenment and the profound influence of a life devoted to spiritual awakening.

Chapter 1: Birth & Early Life: *Bhaba Pagla's story is not just a historical account; it is a living testament to the enduring power of faith, simplicity, and the unyielding pursuit of spiritual awakening.*

In an age where materialism often overshadows the quest for meaning, Bhaba Pagla's narrative invites us to reexamine our priorities, encouraging a shift towards inner development and selflessness. His miraculous birth, the manifestations of his divine connection in childhood, and the profound wisdom of his songs—all serve as reminders that there are realms of experience beyond the empirical that continuously shape human consciousness.

Moreover, his reverence for the Divine Mother, his deep meditation and artistic expression at the crematorium, and his transformative interactions with spectral beings transcend cultural and temporal boundaries, offering insights into the universal human experience of seeking connection with the transcendent.

Amidst technological advancements and societal complexities, the life of Bhaba Pagla is a beacon that illuminates a path of compassion, service, and spiritual dedication. It starkly contrasts the pervasive pursuit of transient success, urging us to uncover and cherish the sacrosanct within and all around us. His embodiment of childlike innocence and his ability to find joy and wisdom even in the humblest acts provide a philosophical compass for navigating the tumultuous waters of our times.

This book is an invitation to rediscover the animating spirit behind our existence and to foster a sense of unity with the divine tapestry of life, knowing that beyond our immediate sight lies a more profound reality waiting to be experienced and understood.

Chapter 2: Bhaba Pagla with His Mother returned to their village: *In this brief glance into Bhaba Pagla's life, we glean an invaluable perspective amidst the fervour of modern achievements. Bhaba Pagla's story teaches us that the journey of self-discovery often diverges from the well-trodden path of education and societal norms. As his formal schooling ended abruptly to usher in his spiritual pursuits, we are reminded that life's true education transcends the confines of classrooms and textbooks.*

In contemporary times, success is frequently measured by academic credentials and material gains, yet Bhaba Pagla's narrative challenges us to redefine accomplishment. It invites us to seek balance between our worldly responsibilities and spiritual growth. His unorthodox actions—whether seeking solace in the Ganga for his mother or instantly crafting the form of the Divine out of clay—exemplify an innate connection to spirituality that often gets obscured in today's bustling society.

Perhaps the greatest takeaway from Bhaba Pagla's life is the affirmation that spiritual enlightenment and harmony are accessible to all, regardless of one's formal education level. His ability to impact those around him and invoke deep reverence and learning illustrates the profound influence of a life devoted to spiritual awakening.

As the author, I present Bhaba Pagla's life not merely as history, but an ongoing dialogue with divinity that beckons us to look beyond the tangible, urging a re-evaluation of what we value and how we grow. May his story be a source of reflection and inspiration, encouraging us to find our own paths to greater wisdom and compassion.

Chapter 3: Udbodhan (The Name of Sarada Maa's House): *In the sacred tapestry of ancient India, the reverence for the feminine divine was not merely symbolic but deeply engrained in the spiritual* *consciousness of the society. Goddess Kali stands as a testament to the profound empowerment of women within Hindu mythology; she is often depicted as the supreme force, wielding immense power that even the mightiest of gods bow to. Her ferocity and autonomy are emblematic of a society that, in its spiritual ideals, honours the strength and sovereignty of the feminine principle.*

The epic narrative of Devi Durga triumphing over the demon Mahishasura illustrates this paradigm, where a woman, a goddess, embodies the ultimate victor over evil. Intriguingly, her empowerment is facilitated through the collective effort of male deities bestowing their weapons upon her, indicating a harmony and acknowledgment of strengths transcending gender.

In the present-day context of Women Empowerment, these ancient depictions resonate with new vigour. They remind us that the concept of empowering women is not a modernistic intervention but a rekindling of an age-old recognition. The narratives of Kali and Durga serve as allegories for the indomitable spirit of womanhood, encouraging the dismantling of patriarchal structures and the celebration of equality.

The dialogue between Bhaba Pagla and Sarada Maa on the unity of Krishna and Kali underscores a holistic perspective where divine qualities are not restricted to gender. It champions a worldview where spiritual insight and unconditional love are the conduits for transcending the dualities of male and female, leading to a state of equilibrium and respect. This ancient wisdom can illuminate contemporary efforts, inspiring society to elevate and harmonize the roles of women in all spheres of life, mirroring the balance depicted in these powerful spiritual figures.

Chapter 4: Bhaba Pagla Returned to Amta and met His Childhood Companions: *In chronicling the life of Bhaba Pagla, it is evident that his journey underscores a universal truth: the human desire to transcend the mundane and connect with the divine. Bhaba Pagla's life, marked by an earnest yearning toward spirituality, teaches us that* *there is a dimension beyond the physical, which he sought to reach with unwavering focus despite the risks and societal incomprehension.*

Today's society, with its relentless pace and emphasis on the material, often neglects this deeper yearning for spiritual communion. Bhaba Pagla's story serves as a poignant reminder that the hunger for spiritual fulfilment is intrinsic to human nature. His quest, while at times enigmatic and extreme, reveals an intense commitment to actualizing his spiritual instincts.

As we grapple with the complexities of modern life, Bhaba Pagla's biography encourages us to honour our internal quest for meaning. His experiences can inspire us to explore our spiritual dimension, to question the nature of our existence, and to remember that the pursuit of a richer, more profound connection with the world is not only possible but essential for our well-being.

While his attempts to escape the physical realm were intense, they also reflect a search for liberation that many of us can relate to, albeit in different forms. As the author, my hope is that Bhaba Pagla's story resonates with those who sense a similar call to spirituality, inspiring them to seek that connection in life-affirming ways within our contemporary context.

Chapter 5: Oh, Mother (Almighty Goddess), You want to shackle a Dear of the Forest: *As we delve into the life of Bhaba Pagla, we confront the timeless debate between spiritual freedom and the constraints imposed by worldly existence. Bhaba Pagla's poignant song about the deer in the forest exemplifies his unwavering belief that real freedom cannot be tethered by materialistic ties or confined within the boundaries of societal expectations.*

In our modern society, where consumerism and the quest for monetary success often dominate, Bhaba Pagla's attitude acts as a catalyst for introspection. His message encourages a reorientation towards intrinsic values rather than extrinsic rewards. His life challenges us to consider whether we are neglecting our spiritual well-being in the relentless pursuit of material comforts.

Bhaba Pagla's actions and compositions remind us that spiritual fulfillment and artistic expression are often at odds with the commodification of daily life. His ability to find solace and a sense of purpose in his devotion to the Divine suggests that it is possible to live a life of contentment and dignity without succumbing to materialistic pressures.

Moreover, Bhaba Pagla's experiences underline the importance of authenticity and commitment to one's principles—a lesson that holds particular relevance today as society grapples with issues of integrity and ethical conduct. As an author outlining his biography, I invite readers to reflect on how Bhaba Pagla's legacy can influence our present-day journey towards a more spiritually attuned and authentic life.

Chapter 6: The Temple of 'Kali' (Goddess) at Amta: *In chronicling the exceptional life of Bhaba Pagla, one cannot help but marvel at the profound intersection of passionate spirituality and cultural exuberance that marks his story. His musical group, free from religious barriers and composed of Hindu and Muslim students alike, is emblematic of inclusivity—a salient lesson for our modern, fragmented society. With his music transcending the lines of faith, Bhaba Pagla championed a message of unity in diversity, harmony, and the universal pursuit of the divine.*

The construction of the temple of Kali, though fraught with familial doubt, perseverance, and divine intercession, stands as a testament to the resilience of faith. It is a physical homage that signifies the immutable presence of spiritual dedication amidst worldly uncertainty.

Bhaba Pagla's life, dedicated to spirituality and the arts, encourages us to recognize the intrinsic value of creative and devotional practices in a world increasingly driven by material gain and practicality. His example inspires a wholesome integration of cultural enrichment with inner growth.

It has been a privilege for me to witness how his philosophy and actions, steeped in authenticity and empathy, resonate in today's context. His legacy serves as a clarion call for each of us to explore the depths of our potential, pushing us towards a convergence of genuine artistic expression, spiritual exploration, and social integrity. Bhaba Pagla's annual festival, infused with music and communal oneness, ultimately shows us that spirituality and cultural vibrancy are not relics of the past but are ever-relevant foundations for fostering a connected and uplifted humanity.

Chapter 7: The Hindu Festival (The worship by dancing): *The myriad experiences of Bhaba Pagla, as detailed in his biography, offer an array of lessons that align with profound truths applicable in our contemporary world. Bhaba Pagla's message of non-violence, compassion, and the transformative power of faith resonates with the values we hold dear today.*

In an era defined by divisions, Bhaba Pagla's all-embracing approach transcends boundaries, embodying the conviction that spirituality can unite where differences may divide. His commitment to a practice devoid of animal sacrifice casts a light on the importance of non-harm and mindfulness in all aspects of life, including our cultural and religious expressions.

Furthermore, Pagla's profound interactions illustrate the potential of human consciousness both to touch and to be touched by the divine. His life demonstrates that earnest devotion can lead to extraordinary occurrences and inspire change in others, even those who may be feared or judged by society.

As the author capturing the essence of Bhaba Pagla, I am struck by the timeless applicability of his teachings. His advocacy for inner transformation over external attraction remains a compelling guidepost for nurturing a deeper sense of being. Bhaba Pagla's life is a reminder to us all that the search for the sacred within and among us can be a unifying and elevating journey, one that can heal, inspire and transcend the mundane realms of existence in our quest for a greater connection with the world and the divine.

Chapter 8: Familial Milestones and Divine Encounters: *In the present societal context, the intersection of familial responsibilities, devoted religious practice, and the evolving aspect of modern life presents a compelling narrative. The theme of taking up family responsibilities alongside the path of devotion and religion is particularly significant in today's age when there is a discernible tendency among the younger generation to defer or opt out of marriage. It is within the backdrop of this evolving social landscape that the poignant story of Bhaba Pagla emerges, offering a narrative that resonates with contemporary societal nuances.*

The compelling portrayal of Bhaba Pagla's dedication to spiritual practice and the concurrent assumption of familial responsibilities offers valuable insights into the multifaceted nature of individual decisions and societal roles. It highlights the enduring significance of familial duty and the complexities of navigating spiritual and familial realms in a modern context. This exploration serves to inspire reflection on the evolving dynamics of family, devotion, and personal choices within the context of contemporary societal trends, evoking contemplation on the interplay of tradition and modernity in shaping individual paths and societal conventions.

Chapter 9: The Golden Stick: *The life and legends of Bhaba Pagla, particularly the story of his golden stick, resonate with timeless truths that are pertinent in our contemporary society. His golden stick, rich in symbolism, stands as a powerful emblem of the transformative impact of spirituality, faith, and the potential for redemption in even the grimmest of circumstances.*

In our modern context, the tale of the golden stick invites us to consider the protective and healing power of our own convictions and values. Bhaba Pagla's encounters with both foes and followers alike reveal that true security and influence do not stem from material possessions or external shows of force, but from an inner strength rooted in a sense of higher purpose and integrity.

What Bhaba Pagla embodies through his golden stick—a symbol of divine power and guidance—is the idea that our personal and collective well-being hinges not on physical defences but on the cultivation of spiritual resilience and the compassionate treatment of others. His ability to transform hardened criminals into devotees without a single act of violence speaks to the potent force of nonviolent resolution and the capacity of empathy to drive transformative change.

Delving into his storied past, I present Bhaba Pagla's life as a testament to the power of spiritual presence and action, and an illustration of how we can navigate our world with grace, dignity, and a profound belief in the virtues we uphold. May his story inspire a reassessment of the true sources of influence and protection in our lives, encouraging each of us to discover and wield our unique 'golden sticks'—our core values—with intention and benevolence.

Chapter 10: Ram Prashad Maha Prashad Great Holy Meal: *The chapter "Ram Prashad Maha Prashad Great Holy Meal" depicts a profound spiritual journey of Bhaba Pagla and his companions to the dwelling place of Ram Prasad, guided by mystical occurrences and encounters with divine figures. The chapter also highlights the deep influence of spiritual music and the symbolic significance of offering oneself as a holy meal.*

In the modern societal context, this chapter resonates with the timeless quest for spiritual connection and the profound impact of devotional music. It reflects the enduring human yearning for mystical experiences and encounters with the divine. The journey to the sacred dwelling place of Ram Prasad portrays the universal human desire to seek guidance and inspiration from spiritual figures and the reverence for ancient wisdom.

The symbolic concept of offering oneself as a holy meal, as illustrated by Bhaba Pagla declaring himself as 'Ram Prasad' and 'Maha Prasad', holds a metaphorical significance in modern society. It echoes the idea of selfless devotion and the transcendence of personal desires through spiritual dedication, offering a profound parallel to the value of selflessness and spiritual mindfulness in contemporary life.

Overall, the chapter captures the timeless themes of spiritual quest, divine encounters, and the transformative power of devotional music, offering valuable insights into the enduring significance of spiritual pursuits and the universal human aspiration for connection with the divine in the modern societal context.

Chapter 11: Episode in Tangile: *The chapter "Episode in Tangile" narrates a series of remarkable episodes depicting Bhaba Pagla's encounters, spiritual experiences, and the profound impact he had on individuals during a tumultuous period in Indian history. It symbolizes the enduring influence of spiritual leaders and the transformative power of faith.*

In the context of modern society, this chapter illuminates the timeless quest for spiritual enlightenment, divine experiences, and the unwavering devotion of individuals towards spiritual figures. It underscores the deep impact of spiritual guidance and the enduring significance of faith in facing societal challenges.

The episodes reflect the universal human yearning for spiritual connection and the transformative influence of spiritual experiences on individuals. The profound impact of Bhaba Pagla's presence on individuals highlights the enduring human aspiration for spiritual guidance and the inner search for meaning amidst societal upheavals.

Overall, the chapter offers valuable insights into the timeless themes of spiritual faith, divine experiences, and transformative influence, resonating with the enduring significance of spiritual guidance and the unwavering devotion of individuals in the modern societal context.

Chapter 12: Welcome Invitation by Nawab of Murshidabad: *The captivating journey of Bhaba Pagla's interactions with the Nawab of Murshidabad and the people around him offers* *profound insights and timeless lessons that resonate with contemporary society. The Nawab's curiosity to meet Bhaba Pagla, drawn by his philanthropy, equal sympathy towards all, and talents in singing and music, reflects the universal human yearning for connection with extraordinary individuals. Bhaba Pagla's refusal to follow the Nawab's initial letter of invitation, instead choosing to use the money to feed people, highlights his unconventional and selfless approach, emphasizing the importance of compassionate action over formalities.*

The symbolic incidents involving the malfunctioning car and the merchant's departure without seeking permission from Bhaba Pagla emphasize the profound impact of simple acts of courtesy and respect, serving as valuable reminders of the significance of humility and reverence in human interactions. Furthermore, Bhaba Pagla's deep connection with those around him, evident in his endearing reference to the Nawab as 'my son' and his ability to touch hearts with just a few words, reflects the universal need for authentic and empathetic relationships, irrespective of social or religious differences.

The unexpected spiritual disturbance experienced by Bhaba Pagla, coinciding with riots in Kolkata, conveys a powerful message about the interconnectedness of spiritual energy and events in the world, serving as a timeless reminder of the subtle yet profound influence of spiritual fervour on societal harmony. Finally, Bhaba Pagla's use of humour and riddles to uplift followers underscores the enduring relevance of joy, laughter, and thought-provoking wisdom in fostering positivity and understanding in human interactions.

The extraordinary life and teachings of Bhaba Pagla continue to offer invaluable lessons for modern society, including the importance of selfless compassion, humility, authentic relationships, spiritual awareness, and the transformative power of humour and wisdom in fostering unity and harmony among diverse communities and individuals.

Chapter 13: A Great Poet of Unification: *The transformative narrative of Bhaba Pagla's intervention in Garparah provides a* *powerful testament to his ability to transcend religious and communal divides, offering invaluable lessons with profound relevance in modern society. Amidst the backdrop of communal tension and potential conflict, his divine influence effectively dissolved hatred and suspicion, fostering an atmosphere of unity and understanding. Bhaba Pagla's approach to resolving the tense situation exemplifies the timeless principles of empathy, wisdom, and inclusivity, serving as a striking reminder of the critical need for peacemakers and unifiers in today's interconnected world.*

Bhaba Pagla's adept use of humour and wisdom to disarm tensions and bridge communal divides serves as a poignant reminder of the transformative power of compassion and understanding in resolving conflicts and fostering unity. His emphasis on the shared linguistic and cultural threads that unite communities, irrespective of faith, resonates with the modern quest for inclusivity and acceptance in diverse societies. Furthermore, Bhaba Pagla's insightful teachings on love, unity, and the true essence of spiritual worship offer profound guidance for navigating contemporary societal challenges marked by divisive rhetoric and conflicts.

Through his teachings on yoga, sacrifice, and spirituality, Bhaba Pagla urges introspection and a shift from material representations to internalized spiritual connections, offering a timeless message of transcending superficial divisions to embrace shared humanity.

Bhaba Pagla's ability to unite and uplift the people of Garparah through his profound teachings and presence underscores the timeless relevance of compassion, unity, and wisdom in addressing contemporary societal challenges and fostering a world marked by understanding, empathy, and universal love.

Chapter 14: The Rising in the East and Setting in the West: *The profound narrative of Bhaba Pagla's transition from East Bengal to West Bengal reflects both the challenges and the enduring resilience of the human spirit in the face of historical upheaval. The tumultuous events following Partition and the poignant departure from Amta underscore the timeless themes of displacement, sacrifice, and the* *unwavering commitment to spiritual transformation in the most trying circumstances, drawing notable parallels with contemporary societal challenges.*

The narrative captures the poignant legacy of communal division and displacement following Partition, manifesting in the persecution of Hindus and the disruptive impact on the cultural fabric of the region. The visionary leadership of Bhaba Pagla amid these adversities serves as a timeless embodiment of resilience and spiritual commitment in fostering unity and compassion in the face of societal disintegration and conflict, resonating with the modern quest for interfaith harmony and social cohesion.

Bhaba Pagla's departure from Amta, marked by poignant encounters with perplexing events and poignant interactions with devoted disciples, reflects the universal human experience of responding to adversity with grace, resilience, and introspection. The departure also represents the exploration of new beginnings in unfamiliar territories, akin to the contemporary challenges of migration, resettlement, and cultural adaptation, emphasizing the enduring significance of spiritual guidance and community solidarity in navigating such transitions.

The remarkable events of Bhaba Pagla's transition from East Bengal to West Bengal serve as a powerful testament to the enduring capacity of the human spirit to triumph over adversity, fostering hope, unity, and spiritual transformation in the face of historical turmoil and societal challenges.

Concluding Remarks: *In the concluding phase of Bhaba Pagla's journey, we witness the encompassing tapestry of history unfold, wrought with moments that echo the dichotomy of human existence—of joy and sorrow, virtue, and ignominy. The narrative traverses through the violent upheavals that scarred the Indian subcontinent, with the malevolent forces of foreign invaders and internal conflicts leaving indelible marks. In the aftermath of the partition, the narrative delves deep into the anguish and* *loss experienced by the people, as the once-holy land of unity found itself severed, stained with the blood of its children.*

As Bhaba Pagla embarks on a new chapter in West Bengal, the narrative encapsulates the essence of his ambition—a garden of spirituality that sprouts the seeds of unity, bridging the East Bengalis of Pakistan with the people of West Bengal, India. This symbolic endeavour embodies the timeless quest for a harmonious coexistence, inspiring us to reflect on the enduring power of spiritual leadership and the possibility of reconciliation in the wake of historical pain and division.

In this way, Bhaba Pagla's journey stands as a singular phenomenon in India's spiritual history, weaving together the threads of compassion, resilience, and the timeless pursuit of unity against the backdrop of a tumultuous era.

I present Bhaba Pagla's life not merely as history but an ongoing dialogue with divinity that beckons us to look beyond the tangible, urging a re-evaluation of what we value and how we grow. May his story be a source of reflection and inspiration, encouraging us to find our own paths to greater wisdom and compassion.

****

Reading of Synonyms Chapterwise

Chapter-1

1. Verdant – Green
2. Tranquil – Calm
3. Venerated – Respected
4. Revered – Glorified
5. Ushered – Began
6. Impending – Approaching
   That Will Happen.
7. Encounter – To Meet, To Face.
8. Somber – Depressing, Bad Situation.
9. Discerned - Felt
10. Perilous – Risky
11. Incarnation – Avatar
12. Divine Consort – Divine Companion
13. Glimse – Quick Look
14. Insinuated – Remarked
15. Grapple – Try To Solve
16. Intriguingly – Interestingly
17. Crisply – Angrily
18. Muddle – Puzzle
19. Perceive – Graspe, Discern, Understand.
20. Delved – Involved For Searching.

21. Conceited – Boastful

22. Impoverished – Poor

Chapter-2

1. Poignant – Distressful, Upsetting
2. Solace – Pacification
3. Rivaled – Competed
4. Implored – Requested To Ask
5. Stone Apple Tree – Bael Tree
6. Reverence – Respect
7. Prank – Joke
8. Embarked – Started
9. Peers – Companions

Chapter-3

1. Odyssey – Journey
2. Exuberance – Enthusiasm
3. Intrigued – Interested
4. Demeanour – Manner, Attitude
5. Encapsulate – Summarize
6. Tapestry – Varieties
7. Deities – Gods and Goddesses
8. Serenaded – Made Listen to Sing A Song
9. Pondered – Would Think
10. Attuned – Made Tune, Made Similar Rythm
11. Revered – Respected
12. Turmoil – Bad Situation
13. Solace – Peace

14. Musing – Thought for a Period
15. Mundane – Domestic
16. Reminisced – Remembered
17. Cherished – Desired
18. Fervour – Encouragement
19. Anbiance – Atmosphere
20. Profound – Grave, Deep
21. Reveal – Express
22. Seclusion – Lonely Place, Solitude

Chapter-4

1. Cherish – To Feel Love
2. Delectable – Tasty
3. Demeanour – Behaviour
4. Emanate – Produce, Grow
5. Contemplative – Thoughtful.
6. Enigmatic – Mysterious
7. Implored – Requested
8. Strolling – Walking
9. Peers – Companions
10. Moniker – Nick Name
11. Endearment – Soft Words
12. Secluded – Stayed Alone
13. Succumbed – Died Down
14. Disdain – Neglect
15. Revelation – Expression of Truth
16. Grappling – Struggling
17. Slumber – Deep Sleep

Chapter-5

1. Errands – Buying Something from a Shop
2. Interrupted – Discontinued
3. Testament – Last Will
4. Luxuriated – Enjoyed as a Luxury
5. Concealed – Hid (Covered)
6. Contemplated – Thought, Planned
7. Ambiance – Environment
8. Revered – Respected
9. Epitomized – Symbolized
10. Venerated – Respected, Admired
11. Pondered – Thought and Worried
12. Elicited – Expressed

Chapter- 6

1. Dimming – Obscures Fade, Feeble
2. Discerning – Approval, Deciding
3. Culminating – Finalizing
4. Acquiescing – Accepting Without Argument
5. Venerate – Respect
6. Contemplate – Think

Chapter-7

1. Adorned – Decorated
2. Embellishment – Ornamented
3. Commotion – Noise Atmosphere
4. Flustered – Puzzled
5. Exuberance – Cheerfulness, Energetic

6. Contemplation – Thought
7. Eschew – Escape
8. Glimpsed – Looked At Suddenly
9. Impetuousness – To Pass Remark Suddenly without Thinking
10. Unwary – Thoughtless
11. Purported – Assumed
12. Indelible – That Cannot Be Removed
13. Nefarious – Ugly
14. Malice – Grudge

Chapter-8

1. Poignant – Painful
2. Enigmatic – Mysterious
3. Interwoven – Interconnected
4. Punctuated – Strengthened
5. Delved – Searched
6. Elucidate – To Explain
7. Epitomizing – Exemplifying to Make Ideal

Chapter-9

1. Discerning – Judging
2. Obstinate – Stubborn, Disobedient
3. Defiant – Adamant
4. Embellished – Decorated
5. Volition – Desire
6. Reminisced – Talked about things that Happened in the Past
7. Covetous – Greedy

8. Redemptive – Saving from Sin and Disease
9. Meek – Gentleness

Chapter-10

1. Relics – Traditionally Past and Present Exists
2. Pondering – Thinking Something
3. Devote – Abandon, Give Up
4. Culminating – Coming to Climax
5. Reminiscence – Memory, Recollection
6. Culinary – Connected to Cooking
7. Metaphors – Imaginative Way

Chapter-11

1. Deeming - Regarding
2. Eavesdropped – Monitored to Spy
3. Nocturnal – Night Time

Chapter- 12

1. Piqued – Awakened
2. Encountered – Came Across, Faced
3. Consent – Permission
4. Esteemed – Valued
5. Whimsy – Impression
6. Thronged – Packed into Jam
7. Glimpse – A Momentary or Partial View
8. Striated – Striped, Banded
9. Emblematic – Symbolic

Chapter- 13

1. Tumultuous – Riotousness, Uproar
2. Simmer – Boiling Condition
3. Loomed – Became Visible
4. Brewed – Fermented, Prepared
5. Fostered – Encouraged
6. Poignantly – Being Impressive
7. Pun – Word Play, Double Meaning
8. Revere – Respect
9. Inadvertently – Unknowingly
10. Mundane – Worldly Affairs
11. Analogy – Likeness, Similarity
12. Predicaments – Difficult, Embarrassing Situation
13. Perpetuate – To Make Continue

Chapter- 14

1. Tapestry – Varieties
2. Upheavals – Turmoil, Unrest
3. Malicious – Hostile, Enmity
4. Malevolent – Evil Minded
5. Jeopardized – Threatened
6. Cleave – Split, Divide
7. Stubbornly – Adamantly
8. Dissipating – Disappearing
9. Asunder – In Two Pieces
10. Abyss – Rift, Gap
11. Shattered – Destroyed, Ruined

12. Turmoil – Tension
13. Abhorrent – Hateful, Disgust
14. Tumultuous – Full of Tumult, Violence & Disturbance
15. Opulence – Wealth and Luxury
16. Qualms – A Feeling of Doubt
17. Satiated – Completely Satisfied
18. Serendipitous – Unexpected
19. Odyssey – Experience of Long Journey in Life